I am Laurie

How Bipolar Disorder Altered My Life

LAURIE JOHNSON

WestBow
PRESS

Scripture taken from the THE HOLY BIBLE, NEW INTERNATIONAL VERSION®.
NIV® Copyright © 1973, 1978, 1984, 2011 by Biblica, Inc.™
Used by permission. All rights reserved worldwide.

WestBow Press books may be ordered through booksellers or by contacting:

WestBow Press
A Division of Thomas Nelson
1663 Liberty Drive
Bloomington, IN 47403
www.westbowpress.com
1-(866) 928-1240

ISBN: 978-1-4497-2813-7 (sc)
ISBN: 978-1-4497-2814-4 (hc)
ISBN: 978-1-4497-2812-0 (e)

Library of Congress Control Number: 2011917916

Printed in the United States of America

WestBow Press rev. date: 10/05/2011

CONTENTS

For Grandma,

Jeremy,

Brent,

and Arnold.

PROLOGUE

Jeremy

My sensitive, compassionate, and talented nephew, Jeremy, took his life on December 8, 2003, at the age of twenty-eight. Jeremy was never diagnosed with bipolar disorder, but since I always felt we shared many similar traits, I wonder if he may have suffered from the same thing I did. After battling bipolar disorder for nearly twenty-seven long years, I received my diagnosis on April 16, 2007. What a difference it might have made if I had known what was wrong four years earlier. Jeremy could have been offered the help he needed, provided he was struggling with the same brain disorder. Since that is no longer possible, there is only one thing to do now. The public needs to be educated, and families must start talking about this illness, which takes one life out of every five people afflicted.

From the age of four or five, I wanted to be a nurse because of my desire to help people. When I was fourteen, my twin nephews, Jason and Jeremy, were born. As they grew, I taught them the alphabet and how to count. I experienced great joy working with the twins, and it inspired me to devote my life to education. Maybe through writing this book I can do both—help and teach.

Recently I realized some of the behaviors I have exhibited since the onset of manic depressive disorder are not what defines who I am as a person. When a person is diagnosed with a mental illness, it is said he *is* bipolar or he *is* schizophrenic. On the other hand, when one is diagnosed with cancer or hepatitis, people are unlikely to say he *is* cancer or hepatitis but rather he *has* cancer or hepatitis. It might simply be semantics, but I believe the power of language helps to either break down or encourage the stigmas associated with mental illness. My preference is to call mental illness "medical illness." It is an inherited disorder that is treatable, like many other medical conditions. The difficulty lies in realizing what is wrong since the symptoms are behavioral. This is where the guilt and shame begin.

As the reader gets acquainted with me by delving into the most private parts of my life, it leaves me vulnerable. I especially want to thank my husband for allowing me to be transparent, as this is also his story. He, too, is left vulnerable as I share of many struggles we faced together at a young age. It is never easy to be completely open, especially when a person is not proud of some of the things he or she has done in life. Since this is a story about the trials I have faced as a person suffering from bipolar disorder, it also involves other relationships I've had. Keep in mind as you read that I am writing only from my perspective, which at times was flawed by the illness and at other times by simply being human. Perceptions and reality can sometimes be two very different things. Remember, there is always another side to every story. I have been as honest as I can be, realizing that there may be things I missed due to a lapse in my memories from the past fifty years.

When I began writing, it was for therapeutic reasons. It was necessary for me to go back after my diagnosis to look at painful experiences to see them differently and allow the healing process to begin. I soon learned that I might also be able to help others with a message of hope through the telling of my story. Somewhere along the way, it became something more. It is now not only a story of hope but also of forgiveness and reconciliation. If writing this book inspires just one person to keep working at his or her marriage, or just one person to quit thinking about ending his or her life, or if just one person comes to the knowledge of the saving grace of the Lord, then the transparency and possibility for personal embarrassment have been worth it.

The title of this book originates from my realization that all of the years of believing I was a failure were due to the fact I *have* manic depressive disorder. *I* am not bipolar; it is something I am afflicted with. When I remember a young woman with big dreams and talents to match before this illness took hold of her life, I like her. Now is the time to recreate her. Here is my story.

CHAPTER 1

Searching for a Knife

For you created my inmost being; you knit me together
in my mother's womb. I praise you because I am fearfully
and wonderfully made; your works are wonderful. I
know that full well. My frame was not hidden from
you when I was made in the secret place. When I was
woven together in the depths of the earth, your eyes saw
my unformed body. All the days ordained for me were
written in your book before one of them came to be.

—Psalm 139:13–16

Jim and I took our church youth group on a swimming excursion in
March of 2007. One of the girls approached us as we were standing
next to each other by the side of the pool and asked, "Are Jim's boobs
bigger than yours?" Now that took me aback. How do you respond
when asked such a question? I'm not sure if I was actually able to say
anything, since it felt as though daggers were piercing my heart. In
reality, Jim and I should have been equally offended by the comment,
but he brushed it off.

Over the next few days, my emotional state descended rapidly.
Unable to shake that awful question from my mind made it hard for me
to sleep. It caused me to wear bulky clothes to cover my inadequacies.
No wonder I hated shopping for swimsuits. I could never find one that
looked how I wanted it to when I put it on. Jim had previously gone
shopping with me as I searched for the perfect swimwear. After trying
on almost all of them my size, he gently said, "You will not find what
you are looking for." He was right. It was impossible to be clothed in
something so skimpy that would hide what was wrong with me.

A few nights after our swimming outing, I experienced something I never had before. Unable to sleep, I walked back and forth from the bedroom toward the garage all night long. It took every bit of strength I could muster to keep from getting a utility knife and carving the word *ugly* across my breasts. Finally I succumbed to the urge, actually walking outside through the snow from the house to the garage. I looked in the tool box for the knife, but it was not in its usual place. I checked other drawers in the tool box. Not readily seeing it, I returned to the kitchen and removed a steak knife from the drawer. Knowing it was dull, I touched it to my arm to test it. Then I made several slicing motions, but it was not sharp enough to easily cut open the skin on my arm. I touched the tip of the knife to my right breast and drew the letter U, so that it would be right side up when someone was facing me. Positioning it to be easily read by others is interesting, since I was not going to allow anyone besides Jim ever to see it. I couldn't make myself use the amount of pressure necessary to pierce the skin with such a dull knife. The *u* would probably not be legible if I had. This would never work.

I may not have been able to resist the urge to mark myself if a wood-burning kit had been available. I envisioned touching the scorching-hot point to my skin, as that could result in a more visible scar without much effort. This action would more than likely cause a permanent mark, which is exactly what I desired in that moment. If there had been a store open at that hour, I'm sure I would have made the trek into town to purchase one. Another recurring yet contradictory thought was that if I was ever to choose breast augmentation, the doctor would never perform it. This brand would prove that I was too unstable. It became a tug-of-war within my mind, but somehow, with these opposing thoughts and the agitation I was experiencing, I lasted the night with nothing more than a few red marks on my arm and breast. These would disappear within a day or two.

I always wondered what might make a person want to cut himself. The best way I can describe what I experienced that night was a sense of self-loathing. Maybe inflicting physical pain would somehow release the emotional anguish I was feeling. Or possibly branding myself in this manner would demonstrate that I was finally believing the message I'd heard repeatedly throughout my life: I was inadequate. I was repulsive, I was ugly. Why would my husband find me attractive when I didn't?

The next morning when Jim awoke, with a hollow look in my eyes, I explained to him how tortured I'd been all night. He stated, "I was afraid you would take it hard. I knew as soon as the words came out of her mouth that I was in for trouble." After all of our years together, he had become aware of what my triggers were, perhaps attributing it to oversensitivity. By morning there were no tears, just a dull emptiness to my expression. Shutting down emotionally because it had become much too painful, I was desperately weary of hurting. Throughout the course of our relationship, I had been highly cautious about what I fully exposed to Jim. I was not proud of the thoughts that invaded my mind periodically, wrestling for hours or even days and weeks at a time without any assistance, except from God. My method of dealing with negative emotions was to hang on by my fingernails until the feelings subsided enough to carry on. My fingernails were becoming brittle and couldn't carry the weight of my burdens any longer without breaking. I needed help.

My beloved husband was obviously concerned. He wanted to take me to a hospital specifically for people in situations like this, but I refused to go. This is why I didn't want to reveal my struggles to anyone. After all, I am not crazy! Then he suggested we both stay home from work. I refused yet again. I would do what I always did, the very thing I *least* wanted to: try to pretend things are normal. If I stayed home, experience told me I would only get worse, if that were even possible. I slowly, robotically, completed the tasks necessary to get ready for work. I arrived right on time, as usual, greeting co-workers with a faked smile. Only capable of fooling them for a short period of time, I was not about to let on that I was not the happy-go-lucky person they believed me to be. It was important to disguise this problem since I am the dependable one. You can always count on Laurie. Throughout the day, Jim phoned repeatedly to make sure I was okay.

My occupation as a Downtown Ambassador is an active one, patrolling the area for graffiti, looking for signs of other mischief, or assisting visitors to town with information and a welcoming smile. Movement is good for brain chemistry. Unable to face the public at first,

I walked the peripheral areas of my beat. As I trudged slowly around the edge, to my amazement, I saw some neatly painted graffiti that said, "You are beautiful." This was unusual, to say the least. Normally, the graffiti I observe is simply a person's initials or something unpleasant and vulgar, often messy. I took a picture of it but did not turn it in to the police department quite yet. I thought I might need to view it again, so I wasn't ready for it to be painted over right away. As I continued walking the perimeter, perhaps a mile away on the opposite side of the zone, there it was again! "You are beautiful" was painted in the same neat writing. I had tears in my eyes as I realized that God was trying to tell me something using the most unlikely source. The next time my husband called, I shared with him that puzzling, yet encouraging, message. Those words were the tourniquet to slow the profuse bleeding of my wounded soul.

After a few days, though still in a weakened state, I could reason clearly enough to know that my reaction to the girl's question was irrational. Most people would likely be offended, but wouldn't resort to such drastic measures as cutting or burning their flesh. How had I, at age forty-six, arrived at such a self-destructive place?

CHAPTER 2

THE SCHOOL YEARS

> Don't let anyone look down on you because you are
> young, but set an example for the believers in speech,
> in life, in love, in faith and in purity.
>
> —1 Timothy 4:12

Three years after I was born in South Dakota, my family moved for a short time to California for my dad's new job. My parents didn't really like big-city life after growing up on their family farms. Six months later, they noticed a tiny little employment ad in the *Los Angeles Times* for a computer programmer position at the University of Montana in Missoula, Montana. Dad applied for it and was hired, so in 1964 our family of eight made the long drive to relocate. Being a little over three and a half years old, I don't have any memories of significance prior to that.

This is a picture of me, prior to moving to Montana.

Family photo. I'm the little one in front.

Mid-1960 Christmas in Missoula.

I was blessed with a very loving and secure home. My parents took us to church every Sunday and taught us to be honest, good people. They were very fair, always spending the same amount of money on each child for birthdays and Christmas. This probably created less sibling rivalry than others might have experienced while growing up. Although there was not a lot of extra money, we never did without anything we truly needed. When the older children began leaving home to start their own lives, it became easier financially for my parents. The younger siblings may have benefited, but I didn't feel spoiled because I always appreciated everything provided for me.

As the youngest of six children born within a seven-year period, my childhood was very happy. When I was in first grade, my oldest sister was in eighth, and we all attended the same school together. I was a good student from the beginning; I loved school and everything about it. Even in the primary grades, I had a competitive streak. I liked being the first to finish my work so I could help the teacher with the next bulletin board and especially delighted in beating the boys in races on the playground. Usually one of the first to be chosen on a team for kickball, I enjoyed all sports. Most people would probably say I was a bit of a tomboy. My gifts one Christmas were a basketball, a football, and a warm-up outfit, since that's what I asked for!

As a young girl, I was sometimes teased by boys who were strangers to me. They would say, "I can't tell if you are a boy or a girl. What are you?" I was tall and skinny for my age, always placed in the middle of the back row in class pictures, and had a pixie haircut. I hadn't given a thought to how short my hair was until I was mistaken for a boy. I didn't mind beating the boys at sports, but I didn't want to *be* a boy. My mom, due to having so many children close together and working full-time, didn't have time to worry about bows and curls every day. Short hair seemed to be the obvious solution, since I was certainly incapable of taking proper care of it at such a young age.

On family vacation.

At some point around first or second grade, my mom noticed a bald spot on my scalp when she was combing my hair. It was probably about the size of a quarter in circumference, located right on the part line, so she immediately took me to the doctor. Mom was afraid that I had something terribly wrong, as she had never experienced anything like this with her other children. I had to endure several shots to my scalp, and my hair grew back completely. The doctor could never tell my mom with any amount of certainty why it happened, but I knew. Embarrassed and believing I would be in trouble if anyone discovered my secret, I never revealed that I regularly twiddled with my hair in that very spot, gradually pulling harder and harder until bits of it would fall out each time. I usually did this at school and remember small clumps of hair ending up on the floor beside my desk. This went on daily until my mom noticed the hairless area. I abruptly stopped once there was evidence because I didn't want to be found out. The painful shots were also a deterrent. To this day, I still don't have any idea what prompted me to pull out my hair, but it does seem strange. A few years later, around the age of ten, I convinced my mom I was ready to care for my hair by myself. She let me grow it out so finally I could look feminine, with long hair, like I was supposed to.

Family photo taken in the backyard out in the country,
1973. I was twelve years old.

My life changed in many ways when my parents decided to move out of town the summer before I entered fifth grade. I was excited because I am a country girl at heart. My dad called me a walking Humane Society since I wanted to take in every stray I found. All of my siblings painfully recall listening to me on road trips, chanting, "Horsey, horsey, I want a horsey!" each time I saw one when I was little. To get the full impact, it must be understood that there were eight people in one vehicle traveling from western Montana to eastern South Dakota to visit relatives each summer. My brothers and sisters have a very good idea how many horses there are across these two large states. Living in the country allowed me to finally realize my dream of having my own horse. Boots was a big, beautiful, black Tennessee Walker/American Saddlebred horse with a white blaze on his nose and three white socks. For me, it was love at first sight. For my brothers and sisters, it meant peace and quiet in the car.

Because of the move, I joined 4-H, had a menagerie of other farm animals, and learned how to garden. I would choose outdoor work any day over housework. I took cooking and sewing projects in 4-H as well but did not enjoy sewing. Helping me sew was one of the few times my mom lost her patience with me. I was not interested in becoming a seamstress, but we finally struggled through my projects. After all of the hard work, someone used a pencil to poke holes in the pillow I'd made prior to it being judged at the county fair. I was unable to understand why someone would be so malicious, but of one thing I was sure—it couldn't be that they felt it might beat their entry. It certainly wasn't that nice, but I would have liked to take it home the way I brought it. My pillow received a second place ribbon because the fabric was soiled and had holes in it. Unbelievable!

I loved our new church. My relationship with God became real for me in a fifth-grade Sunday school class, which is what I am most thankful for during this time in my life. Mrs. Reich had a way of helping us understand the nature of God and how He wanted us to know Him and rely on Him. How important these things would become as events unfolded in my life.

School was not quite as much fun for me where we now lived, however. I did not fit in as well and literally counted down the time until I could go to high school. Four years is a dreadfully long time to wait for a child. The kids were a lot rougher there. Girls had fistfights on the playground, a first-grade boy was suspended from school, and a girl in my class was obviously pregnant at our eighth-grade graduation ceremony. These things didn't happen at my old school in the early '70s. Being trapped there each day always made me feel on edge, because I never knew if I would be the one ostracized that day. Just attempting to fly under the radar was my plan of survival.

One day during sixth grade, a friend of mine and I decided to walk to school. We left really early since it was at least a six-mile journey if we used the railroad tracks as a shortcut. I am a bit surprised our parents let us do this, especially since we had to cross a trestle over the river. Mom and Dad didn't know that in the past, we had purposefully watched for a train to come so we could climb down underneath the tracks to sit on the concrete supports as it flew by over our heads. The whole thing would shake and was extremely loud. When I think back, I would have been *so* angry if my kids had done that. Although my friend and I left with ample time to arrive at school, we dawdled a bit, so it was taking too long to get there. Eventually we decided we better run the last two miles or so to get to school before the tardy bell rang. My poor friend had a hard time keeping up with me, but I didn't want to arrive late, so I was practically dragging her along. I was afraid my parents would never let me do anything like this again and greatly despised being in trouble.

As the day continued, we had a reading assignment and questions to answer for history class. It had to be completed within a certain time frame. My vision was becoming blurred, and I couldn't read. No matter how hard I tried to focus, I simply could not see the words on the page. I started to panic because I wanted to do well on my schoolwork. Then as I looked at my classmates, the left half of their faces were blacked out. My right hand also started to go numb. In a panic, I raised my hand, and without waiting for the teacher to call on me, I said, "I can't read this, I can't read this!" The teacher came up beside me and asked me what was wrong. I told her I couldn't get the words in focus. They would disappear no matter how hard I tried to see them. I was immediately taken to the nurse's office, and the school called my mom. As I waited for her to drive from work all the way out to the country school, my friends came to see me in the office. They started laughing at me as I attempted to answer their questions. Apparently I was speaking gibberish. I was really nervous because I didn't understand what was happening to me.

By the time I was on the way to see the doctor with my mom, I began to get an excruciating headache. It was a sunny day, and I couldn't stand to keep my eyes open. The doctor's diagnosis was a migraine headache. I had several more of these later on, which were exercise or diet induced. It would happen due to strenuous activity after a month or so break from training for high school or college distance races or from eating certain foods, such as chocolate, to excess. I learned to adjust my lifestyle to avoid these headaches, because they literally incapacitated me, resulting in an entire day of misery.

Junior high is an interesting time for all kids and can be very difficult, even without transferring to a new school. I matured late physically and was teased by one person in particular nearly every day about my small breasts. In retrospect, I think this boy actually had a crush on me, and I did consider him a friend. I laughed along with the taunting, but it deeply hurt. Thankfully some other girls my age moved from town to the same subdivision, and we had many things in common. If not for them, a loving home, my animals, and summer vacation, life would have seemed unbearable.

Finally the time came to enter high school. I could start over, make new friends, and be whoever I wanted to be. I did not struggle with depression but now wonder if there weren't some signs of manic behavior at that time. Usually manic depressive disorder, now commonly called bipolar disorder, is noticed and often misdiagnosed when a person has his first deep depression. Since the manic state can actually be intoxicating, most people do not recognize or seek treatment for it. It feels as though you can accomplish anything, and usually do, so it does not seem problematic. I certainly didn't notice anything wrong while in high school, since that's when I had many of my happiest times. I was successful academically and in sports, had many friends, attended church, and felt very fulfilled.

My grade point average was nearly a 4.0. Though I was not completely obsessive about it, I avoided some courses such as physics and calculus since I feared *not* getting an A. Although a high grade point average was important to me, I wanted to put my energies into other areas of my life too. I ended up doing well enough to get an academic scholarship to a state school.

Extremely driven and confident, especially in my chosen sport of distance running, I held state records in the mile and two-mile. I also possessed numerous individual state titles in both cross country and track. No female in Montana had ever broken the elusive five-minute mile barrier until I did as a sophomore. I worked very hard to excel and wouldn't accept anything but the best effort from myself. Lauri, a former competitor and later a college teammate of mine, told me she had always been so impressed I could push myself to a personal best time even if I lapped the entire field of runners. She was a very gifted runner but commented how difficult that was for her without stiff competition.

First place at the state cross country meet, freshman year, 1975.

Lauri certainly showed me what she was capable of at the state track meet my freshman year of high school. I had been undefeated during the entire season in both of my events, the mile and 880-yard run. Lauri was a senior. After having been beaten by me at the state cross country meet in the fall and again in a spring track meet, she was bent on finishing her high school career with a victory. Her experience definitely paid off as she out-maneuvered me in the finals for the mile. I learned some valuable racing strategies from that experience, and she deserved the win. We both annihilated the existing state record and finished a mere half-second apart.

Later in the meet, we would race again in the half mile. Also in the line-up was a very good freshman runner from another school, whom I also considered a friend. I held the lead going into the final turn. Every good distance runner knows, if you are able to hold the other person off on the corner, they will have to run farther than you. She attempted to pass me, so I sped up, causing her to cover more ground. The other runner's vision was poor, and she ran without her glasses. On previous occasions, she had nearly tripped me by stepping on my heels from behind, so I was always a bit nervous about falling whenever I raced against her. Well, of course, the state meet would be the time for a tripping incident to occur. She cut in without having a running stride lead on me, and I ended up stepping with one foot to the inside of the track, barely catching myself before taking a tumble. At that point she took the lead, and I struggled to get my head back in the race. When we crossed the finish line, she was barely ahead of me, with Lauri, the mile champion, in third place. Breathless, my friend turned to me and apologized for tripping me. We both knew exactly what had happened. A red flag was raised on the corner where the incident happened, and I felt bad that she would be disqualified, since I knew it was unintentional.

A moment later, my coach informed me that *I* had been disqualified! I was in disbelief. At first I wondered if I was disqualified for stepping off the track when I was tripped. My coach filed a complaint, and even Lauri went to the officials on her own to tell them what she had seen. They refused to change the ruling. The official on the corner said the other runner had passed me and then as I tried to move outside to pass her again, I caught her foot and tripped her. That would be a stupid strategy on the corner. If she had truly passed me, I would have waited until the final stretch to make my move for a sprint to the finish. Also, if she'd had a full running stride on me in order to pass safely and move to the rail, I would not have been able to clip her back foot as I went to the outside. If my momentum was going toward the right in order to pass, how could I step off and nearly fall to the inside of the track on my left? None of it made any sense. In my mind, the goal was to hold her off, making her cover more ground so I would easily be able to out sprint her down the stretch. I had not even entertained the idea to go around to pass her under those circumstances.

After the pre-meet expectations in which I could score as many as twenty points at the state meet my freshman year, I ended up with eight points and a disqualification. The hardest part about it was watching my friend smiling up on the awards stand, bending down to receive my medal. I couldn't figure out how she could even accept it, knowing it didn't rightfully belong to her. It was easy to convince myself that I wouldn't have taken the medal if the situation had been reversed. In retrospect, as a freshman in high school, I'm not so sure I would have had the maturity to make that choice, either.

The second hardest part was dealing with the embarrassment of being disqualified. Would people think I had tripped her on purpose to try to win? I lost some sleep that night, waiting for what the newspaper would report about it. I had a difficult time letting this disappointment go after training so hard and having such high expectations. Part of my overreaction may have been due to being young and immature, while part of it may have been the beginnings of the disorder, though I'm not exactly sure. Accepting defeat gracefully, even when the circumstances seem unfair, is an important learned skill, since there are certainly many other things that can happen in life that are much worse.

My dad was very proud of me for my success in running and would embarrass me by telling strangers about my most recent victories. Mom and Dad took me out to dinner at a nice steak house to celebrate when I broke five minutes in the mile for the first time. He told the waitress all about it, making me blush, though it can't help but make a daughter feel good to know her parents are proud of her.

Dad also had a special way of encouraging me when I was tired of the grind from constantly working out. He would gently remind me of all the amazing experiences I'd enjoyed because of running. I had visited a variety of places and met so many wonderful people, not to mention the satisfaction that came from accomplishing goals I had set for myself. With some encouragement from the girls' basketball coach, combined with feeling an immense amount of pressure as a runner, I almost switched to basketball during the fall of my sophomore year. Ultimately I decided against it. This created a bit of tension between the two coaches for a short time. I was pleased I stayed with running, and my second year of high school was the most successful of all four years. I won state titles in cross country, both the mile and half mile in track, and set the state record in the mile.

Running at a cross country meet for Sentinel High School.

After I broke five minutes in the mile for the first time,
this was posted on top of my high school.

I've often heard it said that distance running is 95 percent mental, and I believe it. Of one thing I am certain: if you think you *can't* accomplish something, you won't. I was as tough as they come and did not entertain the idea that I was going to lose. In the fall of my undefeated junior year, I broke a bone in my foot with one week left in the cross country season. I was on crutches until it was time to warm up for my race at the state meet. We had a shot at our first team trophy in the history of the school, so I decided to run on my injured foot. Placing eighth, it was easily my poorest finish at any high school race, even nationals. Afterward, I had dry heaves while sitting on the grass near the finish line due to the pain. It was worth spending the next several weeks on crutches, because we finished third place as a team that year and brought home the elusive trophy. Later, at a school assembly, our girl's cross country team was recognized for our high finish at state. There is a photo in the yearbook of the entire team using crutches to parade out on the gym floor, showing how we always stuck together as a team through thick and thin.

Sentinel girls' cross country team with third-place trophy at the state meet my junior year, 1977.

Sleeping was difficult for me the night before any meet but especially if it was an important race. Whenever I went to a state, regional, or national meet, I was lucky to sleep at all. I ran the race over and over in my mind but continually tried to relax. The later it became, the more stressed I was, always calculating how many hours I could sleep if I fell asleep immediately. This was a vicious cycle and something I kept to myself. It is typical for someone in a manic state to be unable to quiet their thinking, so this may have been a sign of what was to come. The wheels would not stop turning no matter what.

I attempted to eat the same foods the night before, and the morning of, a meet. I had a ritual of how I warmed up for races and hoped the meet stayed on schedule so it would not throw me off. Heaven forbid my hour-long warmup was cut short a bit, and even worse if it was lengthened, which happened most often. On race day, I frequently managed on far less sleep than is desirable, so the extra exertion was disconcerting. I was becoming very rigid but worked extremely hard not to show it outwardly. Most people who take a sport seriously have routines, but it distressed me a little too much when mine were interrupted.

Another thing I did secretly during this period of time was to awaken early the morning after a meet to see what the newspaper said about me. Oftentimes I was up before the paper arrived at 4:00 a.m. Maybe there would be a photo, but did they catch me grimacing as I crossed the finish line? I was so concerned about being perfect, having my quotes accurate, and not being embarrassed by the potential picture. No matter how much I wanted and needed the sleep, I could not stay in bed until I read the sports page. I would be as quiet as possible so as not to disturb my parents or siblings when I went outside to retrieve it from the box at the end of the driveway. Our metal screen door would rattle no matter how careful I was. I dreaded being found out. After all, I was exhibiting such prideful behavior. I often wondered if my mom and dad were aware of how the paper mysteriously made its way into the house on those occasions. I revealed this to my mom recently, and she did not remember it.

I have always had an interest in the meaning of names, probably because it seems relevant in the Bible. My name means "crown of victory" since it originates from the laurel wreath athletes won in competitions. My mom chose my name, Laurie, simply because she liked it. I always thought God wanted me to be named appropriately because of my running ability. Little did I know how incredibly shallow that interpretation was and what significance my name would have for me in the future.

During high school, I was nearly always introduced as, "Laurie Holm, the runner." If someone failed to add "the runner," the other person would inevitably say, "Oh, you're the runner." It was as if it had become part of my name, even my identity. Quite frankly, I enjoyed the attention and began to expect the positive reinforcement for all of the effort I put forth. It is very dangerous to have your identity tied to what you do rather than to who you are. Later on, this proved nearly fatal for me.

On the cross country team, we all had nicknames. Everyone loved making up new names for me, and I enjoyed the attention. Being tall and thin, they ranged from "Stick," "Pencil," "Pin-body," "Twig," and finally the funniest one, "Twig Pig." This ended up being the favorite of the team after I won a turkey in the Turkey Trot fun run. My mom cooked it for the team, and once they saw how much I could eat and still remain thin, "Twig Pig" it was.

Right after my freshman year in high school, I gave my first and only autograph. I was riding on a Greyhound bus to Coeur d' Alene, Idaho, to attend Camp Lutherhaven with my cousin. The recipient also participated in track and happened to be from a small Montana town. Apparently he knew who I was, but I didn't know him. I was flattered but a bit embarrassed. After all, I was not famous like the people I looked up to in sports and not nearly as fast . . . yet! Mine were lofty goals involving Olympic dreams. I would satisfy some of my ambitions, but many were left unmet.

Friends were very important to me during my high school years, but we did not go out partying on the weekends. The wildest pastime for us was to drive down "the drag" on a few occasions. I would have been too nervous to drive my parents' car there, because the other kids drove a little crazy, hanging out the windows, honking and yelling. We pooled our money, fifty cents each, to help pay the driver for the gas.

19

Due to my self-confidence, I was also a champion of the underdog. There was one instance in particular I will never forget. As a freshman, I rode the bus to school. It was so crowded one day that every seat but one was taken. A classmate of mine was the last to board the bus, so he headed toward the only seat left, which was near the back of the bus. A junior boy sat there alone and didn't want to share it with him. This freshman boy was such a nice kid. He was a bit timid and spoke with a stutter. He wasn't a star athlete, but he was incredibly intelligent. The poor guy asked the older boy if he could sit there, but he refused. Then my classmate asked everyone in the surrounding seats, but they were all filled. The bus was moving along, the driver oblivious to the fact that this young man was getting tossed about.

Well, I happened to be sitting in the very last seat, directly behind the upperclassman, so it became my "duty" to right this wrong. The correct way to handle it would be to alert the bus driver, but as a fourteen-year-old, my intentions were better than my judgment. In my most stern voice, I said, "Let him sit down!" The junior held his place at the aisle edge of the seat. I repeated, "Let him sit down!" He wouldn't budge, so I decided to hit him over the head with the heel of my very heavy snow boot. This happened several more times until he quietly slid over and let my friend take his place in the seat. I was satisfied and went through my day, forgetting all about it.

My parents believed the family should have dinner together each night, and as we were all seated around the table, the phone rang. In those days, most people did not call during the sacred dinner hour, so my dad was less than pleased with the intrusion. His first response to the person on the other end of the line was, "She did *what?*" Then, "She hit him with a *what? A book?*" I slid deeper and deeper into my chair, thinking, *A boot, Dad, a boot.* I just wanted this to be over, but I knew there was no escape. My dad momentarily excused himself from the call and asked me what had happened. With a quivering voice, I explained it, step by step. After all, honesty was the best policy around our house. Dad looked at my brother and asked if that was what happened. He said it was, so my dad proceeded to tell the other father a thing or two about his son bullying my friend. I was in shock! I gradually started to sit up straighter in my chair. When Dad got off the phone, he complained how ridiculous it was that an older boy's dad would call him about that, especially since, in a way, his son had started it. I felt I had dodged a bullet, but I guess it was a case of the lesser of two evils.

The most important aspect of my life is my faith. During my sophomore year, I took an honors English course from a teacher who did not believe in God. We were studying mythology, and she treated the Bible as mythology also. That was the first time I ever considered the Bible could just be a story. She seemed so certain about her convictions that I actually questioned my faith. I continued attending church but was not quite as sure of what I believed as I previously had been.

Also when I was a sophomore, at age sixteen, I finally started my period. I had been extremely thin, with a body fat percentage that often dipped below 10 percent. This caused me to be quite far behind my peers in getting my menstrual cycle. I wasn't aware that was the reason until much later, however, or I may have accepted it better. Believing there was something wrong with me, I didn't want anyone to know I hadn't started my period. Now I was finally a woman. I was embarrassed to change in the locker room with other girls because my breasts were very tiny. I would use a bathroom stall if one was available or hurry as quickly as I could with my back turned to everyone else. Confident in every other way, this was my secret insecurity at that time.

When I was a senior, I was chosen to be an American Field Service (AFS) domestic exchange student to Pennsylvania. Murrysville was twenty miles east of Pittsburgh, so my "mom" recruited me into becoming a Steelers fan. I had my first minor bout with depression while there but thought it was only homesickness. It lasted a few months, and it was probably more than just pining for home. I had a calendar on the wall of my bedroom and marked off the days until I could return home. This depression would affect my choice of a university later on. I wanted to make sure it would be possible to go home for the weekend, and especially holidays, if I chose to do so.

I competed in cross country while in Pennsylvania and was pushed extremely hard in practice since we worked out with the boys' team. That was a first for me. The result was that I set a new course record at every meet until I pulled both Achilles tendons just prior to the state meet. Needless to say, the end result at state was not very good. I took eighteenth place, which seemed ridiculous, even considering my injuries. Mentally, I was really not in it at all, since I had competed at nationals in track the previous August. After my track season was so prolonged, then having moved right into cross country, coupled with the injuries and homesickness, I was just burned out.

When I returned to school on Monday, my government teacher made sure to bring up how I'd done at the state meet. He finished by saying, "Weren't you a state champion in Montana?" I nodded, sheepishly. "Well, we Pennsylvanians sure showed you Montanans how to run, didn't we?" Ouch! I did not answer. Slouching in my chair, my heart sunk, and I felt angry, ashamed, and defeated all rolled into one. Then the boy across the aisle, also a cross country runner, tapped me on the arm and whispered, "We know the truth. Don't worry about him." My teammate's words helped, but they did not erase all of the damage done. I had always liked that teacher, but it became difficult to keep from holding a grudge until that semester was over. Words can be extremely powerful, and these were particularly stinging.

My AFS "parents" attended church, so I continued to go to services and youth group. I had a wonderful cross country teammate and friend, Leigh, who had a very strong relationship with the Lord. Coach Bullock was a Christian too and held an optional team Bible study in his home. I'm not sure if they were aware of what I was going through, but having them in my life at that time was a blessing. My wavering trust in God was given a critical boost. How thankful I am for my parents' consistent church attendance and example, my fifth-grade Sunday school teacher who revealed God's love to me, and my coach and friend who steered me back on course. The influence of these people contributed greatly to why I am alive today.

On my way to the Pennsylvania state cross country championship with Leigh and Mr. Bullock, fall of 1978.

All in all, I led a pretty healthy life as an adolescent. Because of a history of migraine headaches beginning in the sixth grade, I became aware of what triggered them. Wanting to avoid those at all costs, I adjusted my lifestyle. My diet was generally wholesome. I practiced the old adage, "Early to bed, early to rise," and of course exercised. I didn't drink, smoke, or use drugs. I was unaware of how important all of these healthy disciplines would become as I would soon begin a battle more painful than any race or physical workout I'd ever experienced.

CHAPTER 3

FIRST LOVE

Place me like a seal over your heart, like a seal over
your arm; for love is as strong as death, its jealousy
unyielding as the grave. It burns like a blazing fire, like
a mighty flame. Many waters cannot quench love; rivers
cannot wash it away. If one were to give all the wealth of
his house for love, it would be utterly scorned.

—Song of Songs 8:6–7

After graduating from high school, I obtained my first real job.
In junior high, I babysat in order to have spending money and
one time sold magazines to everyone in the neighborhood so I could
purchase my first ten-speed bicycle. I also sold goat's milk until we
moved to town at the end of my sophomore year of high school. It
requires commitment to raise any kind of dairy animal, but I loved
caring for all of my pets. Teaching us to work hard was important,
but my parents also felt between school, running, family activities, and
church, there was not enough time for employment. That was very wise
of them, since everything would have suffered had I been employed
during high school.

I was hired at a fast food restaurant the summer after my senior
year and completed the workouts my new college coach sent to me. After
receiving letters from larger schools such as UCLA and the University of
Houston, I accepted a scholarship at Montana State University for several
reasons. Mr. Eliason, or "Mr. E." as we affectionately called him, was
quite well known in Montana for his coaching ability. His former junior
college team won nationals once, and he consistently produced good
athletes. I would also have some very talented teammates, including
Lauri, who had beaten me in the mile my freshman year, and I believed
we could perform quite well together. Last but not least, after my

difficulties adjusting in Pennsylvania, this seemed like a wise move. I could experience college life away from home, yet it was only a three-hour drive away, so I wouldn't miss Thanksgiving and Christmas with my family again.

Many of my friendships had changed by the time I returned from Pennsylvania at the semester break of my senior year in high school. A couple of my best friends were a year ahead of me, so their absence accounted for much of the difference. Friends who were still there had found other people to fill the void when I left, so it didn't feel the same upon my return. Due to these circumstances, I worked and trained for cross country during the summer after graduation but found myself bored, with little social outlet. Without even thinking, I blurted out to my brother, "Do you have any friends you could introduce me to?" I don't know where that came from, since I was not looking for a boyfriend. After all, I would be leaving for college in a short period of time. I'd never even been in a relationship before, other than the silly junior high type where you're going with someone, but where?

My brother, Jeff, was working in our hometown at the University of Montana cleaning dorms that summer. He had made a friend named Jim who was six foot five and owned a Camaro. I am six feet tall, which is rare for a female distance runner, and it is rarer still for me to feel short compared to others. Jeff mentioned my request to Jim, and he was interested in meeting me. It was decided that the encounter would occur at a co-rec softball game, and I would play for Jim's team. It was not really a date, as we drove separately. It was just an opportunity to check each other out. I was a bit nervous since I had never been so bold as to do something like this, but it turned out to be an enjoyable evening. I like playing softball, Jim was extremely comfortable to be around, and I loved the beautiful silver car!

We met on July 2, 1979, which is when Jim asked me to go out on our first real date. We went to a movie, though I can't remember what it was. On the way into the theater, Jim grabbed my hand. It seemed so natural, and I was amazed how at ease he made me feel. After the movie, I suggested we buy a six-pack to "liven things up." Again, I don't know where that came from, because I was not a drinker and didn't even like the taste of beer. We went up to his parents' house, where Jim still lived, took our beer to the basement, and made out. Everything about the start of this relationship was contrary to my normal way of life. Things certainly became busy after that, as we spent every possible moment together. We could not stand being apart.

Our relationship progressed rapidly, much more so than I ever would have envisioned. After being steadfastly committed to purity until marriage, my standards changed, and I appeared helpless to do anything about it. I had never felt this way about anyone before, and Jim seemed so strong and safe. He was laid back, an oasis of tranquility in my otherwise disciplined life. Prior to my departure for school, Jim asked me to have sex with him just once before going to college. As I think about that, I wonder if it was a way to hold on to me, an extra assurance of commitment since I would be away for an extended period of time. Very nervous and not sure what to do, I posed the question to my sister. She asked me if I loved him. Of course I did. Then it would be okay, she stated.

I left for college that fall, as planned. I missed Jim, but we called and wrote letters. Right away other young men were asking me to go out on dates. Since this was a new experience for me, I was flattered by it but declined. Still, I was struggling with how much intimacy Jim and I shared, and it scared me. I felt I had disappointed God since I lowered my standards of purity, as things had moved along much too quickly for me.

My dating experience had been literally zero before Jim, and I needed to know if I was making the right commitment to the right person. It seemed the focus had been on passion without knowing everything I needed to about him. After all, how can a person really know if she is in love after dating for only two months? With that in mind, I decided to call Jim and describe my feelings. Our conversation was unpleasant, and Jim was hurt. I couldn't be dishonest, however, and needed to slow things down in order to know for sure if he was truly the one. Jim said, "It's them or me" in reference to the guys who wanted to date me. I explained that I didn't want to end it with him but could not in good conscience get to know others behind his back. Though painful, it seemed right at the time. It is nearly impossible to be so involved with someone and then take a step back without some sort of negative result.

Being an athlete at that level meant I routinely missed having my period due to low body fat. I generally would only have two periods each year in between cross country and track seasons. In the back of my mind, I was afraid I might be pregnant without knowing it, even though we had taken precautions during the only time we had been intimate. Every day I looked at my stomach in the mirror to see if I noticed any change. This went on for almost six months before my mind completely rested at ease. I had been apprehensive about going to the doctor to find out for sure, fearing I might actually consider having an abortion due to my goals in running. After all, how could I have a baby, especially at that time of my life, when I was not even dating the father? Not dealing with this situation properly cost me a certain amount of peace on a daily basis but kept me from being directly confronted with making a decision if I had actually become pregnant. This was very unusual for me, as I normally faced difficulties head-on. It may have been due to the fact that I could not even bear to look at a conflict between two of the most important things imaginable at the time: my running career and the life of a baby. The irony is that by not making a decision, in effect I really was. Life would have ultimately won.

The fall cross country season was great and helped me focus my attention elsewhere. The girls on the team were all Christians, and we had a Bible study every Friday night before our meets. One of my teammates even wrote a song with all of our names in it, plus the team verse, "But those who hope in the Lord will renew their strength. They will soar on wings like eagles; they will run and not grow weary, they will walk and not be faint" (Isa. 40:31).

Though high school was wonderful in many ways, my first year of college easily surpassed it. I never had any problems with depression or homesickness, in spite of the situation with Jim. I felt very balanced and had many new friends. I was successfully navigating life on my own while setting personal bests in my events in track and competing in four different national championships throughout the year. One of our trips was to Florida, so we went to Disney World, something I was never able to do as a child. Holly, a teammate who did not qualify for the meet, jokingly asked me to bring home a palm branch for her. I decided it would be funny to surprise her until I had to figure out how to bring a large, fan-shaped branch on the airplane. Getting it off the tree was extremely difficult and probably illegal as well. Since it would not fit into any of my luggage, I sheepishly carried it all the way home as strangers stared at me in each airport. Though tempted, after all I'd gone through up to that point, I was determined not to throw the palm branch away. I sure hope she appreciated it!

On the plane coming home from cross country nationals with Lauri, my freshman year, fall of 1979.

The palm branch for Holly.

During the indoor track season, I was attempting to hit a national qualifying time for the thousand-meter run. It was my last chance for the season with relatively no competition. I did what I was accustomed to and concentrated on pushing myself, using my lap times to motivate me. With one lap to go, all of a sudden a photographer jumped out in front of me. There was no way to avoid her, and we brutally collided. Apparently, with the crowd at the finish line area, she did not realize I was so far out in front and was trying to get into position to take a photo of the pack.

Whenever I've been tripped or have fallen during a race, it has been incredibly difficult to get my focus back. It's almost like going into a little bit of shock. I did the best I could but missed the qualifying mark by a mere four tenths of one second. It is an absolute certainty I would have qualified if not for this mishap. I was already going to nationals in the distance medley relay but no individual events, so of course it was a disappointment. I knew, however, this photographer would feel worse about it than I did, so I sought her out, put my arm around her, and told her not to worry about it a bit. This reaction differed greatly from my handling of the tripping incident at the state meet four years earlier. This could possibly be attributed to maturity and also being in a stable mental place.

Later I found out the officials were going to let me run the race over again at the end of the meet, using "rabbits" to help me stay on pace. Three of my teammates took turns running beside me to keep me going. Believe it or not, I finished in *exactly* the same time as the first race, therefore not qualifying for nationals in the event. Apparently, the meet officials had seen my reaction to the photographer and felt badly I did not qualify. Without my knowledge, they petitioned the governing body, AIAW (the woman's equivalent to the NCAA at the time), into letting me compete at nationals, and it was granted. God was very gracious in allowing this situation to occur. It shows me who I really am during a very calm period of my life, mentally. As important as it is to work hard and do your best, it is character that really counts. Races do not matter as much as people.

Jim and I had only communicated once since breaking up, while I was home for Christmas. I called him, though he did not seem terribly interested in speaking with me. He may have still been pretty hurt or even angry about what I'd chosen. Maybe he was involved with another girl. I never allowed anything serious to develop with anyone while away at college because, fearing I may disappoint God again, I did not want to get myself in the same predicament twice. There was one person on the track and cross country team I chose to date for about six weeks. It lasted that length of time because all of my teammates constantly teased me that I could not seem to stay with anyone more than one or two dates. They figured I would be the last of us to marry and have children. This guy invited me to his house over spring break to meet his parents. I went up there for the first part of the break, but it felt so uncomfortable since he was so shy. Though he was incredibly nice, it was hard to carry on a conversation with him. I found myself comparing him, and anyone else who was interested in me, to Jim because I was still devoted to him. I was beginning to find the answers I felt I needed in order to commit to Jim. I really did love him.

When I came home for the second part of spring break, I called Jim and told him how much I had missed him. I was hoping he would be willing to take a chance on me once again, and he was! He had seen me running in Missoula with the guy I had been dating and realized he still had strong feelings for me. We went to church together, and I was introduced to a very nice man who was close to Jim's family. He said, "Oh, are you from Kalispell?" One of Jim's good friends started laughing. A little surprised that this man didn't know who I was because of my running. I said, "No, I'm from here." I didn't understand what was so hilarious until later. Apparently Jim was dating a girl from Kalispell, so this person thought I had come from there for a visit. I remember feeling very hurt by the fact that Jim's friend found it so funny, and I guess I felt a little jealous, too. This was not terribly fair, however, since I also dated other people while away. Besides, I had been the one to break up with him.

Even though my freshman year was incredibly fun and I was busy in a successful outdoor track season, summer could not arrive soon enough so we could be together. It was the first year I had competed in three full seasons of distance running. As a high school student, I often had extended seasons due to participating in AAU events but never of quite this intensity or length. When I did arrive home, I was ready for a break. With Jim there to distract me, I had a hard time being motivated to train. Again, he was the counterbalance to the intensity that was foremost in my life.

Sometime around mid-summer, I made a decision that would startle everyone. Jim and I decided to get married, and I would be giving up school, running, my scholarship, and my Olympic dreams. Impulsion and poor decision-making ability are prevalent in people with bipolar disorder. With a short break from running, I would have been ready to go again. How could I permanently walk away from what I had been passionate about for so long? I was relinquishing a full-ride scholarship for an entry-level, minimum wage job at a sporting goods store. This is when, at age nineteen, the crazy ride called my life began.

CHAPTER 4

DEVASTATION

Answer me quickly, O Lord; my spirit faints with longing. Do not hide your face from me or I will be like those who go down to the pit. Let the morning bring me word of your unfailing love, for I have put my trust in you. Show me the way I should go, for to you I lift up my soul. Rescue me from my enemies, O Lord, for I hide myself in you. Teach me to do your will, for you are my God; may your good Spirit lead me on level ground. For your name's sake, O Lord, preserve my life; in your righteousness, bring me out of trouble.

—Psalm 143:7–11

In the fall, when I should have been starting my sophomore year of college, I found myself working for a small, local business with few employees, often alone. Jim started spending more time with his friends. None of them had girlfriends, so they were encouraging him to go out to the bars. He decided one weekend night would be reserved for his buddies and one night would be spent with me. The atmosphere at bars is not the best anyway, but Jim was going with a bunch of young, unattached guys. From what Jim had previously told me about some of his friends, I felt I understood why they were at the bars, and it was not to find a nice girl to have a relationship with. I did not care for the arrangement but felt powerless to change anything. I did not protest at first, but before long I became aware that Jim was not always where he said he was. One time he said he couldn't see me because of a family commitment. When we were together the next day, we ran into one of his friends. This person mentioned how much fun they'd had together at a party the night before. Why had Jim not told me where he was? Were there other girls there? If so, why hadn't he invited me to come along with him? It made me wonder what else he might be doing.

Aware that Jim and his friends frequented a bar in a small town outside of Missoula, I began to hate even hearing the name of it. I had never been inside, but on numerous occasions we would drive past it to go visit one of his sisters, and I physically experienced a jabbing pain in my heart and a sick stomach each time. It seems that almost everything stirred up negative emotions in me. For the most part, I did not tell him when these feelings would occur or he would have become weary of listening to me say it several times each day in various circumstances. I did much of my suffering in silence, but sometimes I would punch Jim in the arm. It started out as a playful thing. Eventually it was a way to hurt him for the pain I was beginning to feel. Once the punches became more powerful, fully unleashing my emotions, he would tell me, "Just because I'm big doesn't mean it doesn't hurt me."

One night Jim went to a bachelor party, and I was extremely upset about him going. I did not trust him and especially did not trust his friends, so I could not keep my mind free of the possibilities of what they could be doing. I suspected they might be at one of the guys' apartments, and I was really not feeling stable that night. I had rarely ever had alcohol in my life, but I bought a bottle of cheap wine, sat in the weeds up on the side of the mountain above the apartment, and started drinking. I saw Jim's truck parked down there and envisioned girls inside doing all sorts of things with them. They were certainly in there a long time. At one point, I actually climbed down the hill and jumped into the bed of his truck, careful to curl up into a ball in the corner, hoping he wouldn't see me when he finally came out. My heart was pounding and I was afraid to breathe lest I make any noise, as I heard the rowdy group of guys come out of the apartment. If only I could have made myself invisible. I had made such a mistake. Jim was going to be so mad at me because I would be an embarrassment in front of his friends. Why was I being such a control freak? I didn't know where they would be going and didn't want to be found out. What if they drove miles away and I had to walk back home? The ride would be a chilly one, since the cooler night air had descended, and I was not prepared for it. If they had been drinking, would I be safe riding in the bed of a pick-up truck?

For some reason, after a bit of loud talking, it became quiet again. Did I dare look over the edge of the truck bed? Holding my breath, peeking just over the top, I saw they had all disappeared back into the apartment. Seizing the opportunity, I bounded out of the truck and ran back up the side of the hill as quickly as I could, hoping no one had seen me. Then I sat there and cried. A short while later, Jim and all of his friends came back out, got into vehicles, and took off. I missed my opportunity to see where they were going, and it just about drove me insane since I couldn't control this situation. I don't know what they did after that or where they went, but there hadn't been any girls in the apartment. Later, after admitting what I'd done, I asked Jim why they went back inside. "To watch a movie for the second time," he replied. I knew what kind. After all, it *was* a bachelor party.

My parents had stressed during my childhood that honesty was of utmost importance. If we were caught doing something wrong, there would be a punishment, but if we lied about it, the penalty was much worse. I had the mistaken notion that's how everyone lived, so I simply could not understand Jim's behavior at times. I thought he must really be hiding something, and my mind went crazy thinking about it. I doubted him so much, I actually made an appointment to be tested for sexually transmitted diseases, which came out negative. The more I questioned Jim, the more secretive he was, and it became a vicious cycle. We originally had set a wedding date of December 31, and the bridesmaids' dresses were already purchased. Jim decided he wasn't quite ready and wanted to wait until Valentine's Day. Then Valentine's Day was going to be too soon for him, so we had no date set . . . maybe the next summer.

After giving up all of my dreams, it seemed I had walked into a nightmare. I begged Jim to let me go if he truly didn't want to be with me. For some reason, I couldn't bring myself to make that decision on my own but wanted him to just tell me whether he wanted me or not. He always assured me that he wanted us to be together, but his actions seemed to say otherwise. I believed I had disappointed my parents, so I chose not to discuss this problem with them. My friends were all away at college, and I had no friends at my current job. With no support system, I became despondent to the point of suicide. After being a very outgoing, confident person, I hardly ever smiled that fall. Our relationship had deteriorated so much that I decided to go back to what I knew best. I called my college coach and made plans to return to school in January. The wedding was postponed indefinitely, and I tried to give the engagement ring back. Jim became a bit insecure and wanted me to continue wearing the ring while away at school. He was insistent, so I agreed.

I was greeted back at school with open arms, and in fact, my coach petitioned to get my scholarship back. By some miracle it was granted, and I should have been back on track. I tried to be disciplined and enthusiastic but was pretty damaged at the time and terribly dependent on Jim. I was longing to be with him, and we spent many hours on the phone. After all, we were still engaged; I was just trying to clear my head. There were guys asking me out, but I held true to Jim and declined. There was even one very persistent fellow who owned a Corvette, and I did like sports cars!

I only completed winter session of my sophomore year in college. Jim was pleading with me to come home, and I had a hard time adjusting to life without him. Things would be different now, much better. Much to my coach's and parents' chagrin, I impulsively gave up my scholarship once again to be with Jim and left school at spring break. It was only days after I returned home that I jokingly grabbed his wallet and said, "Let's see what's in here." I am unsure of what prompted me. I was so thrilled to be home and back with the love of my life. I was absolutely stunned when I found a female name and phone number on a scrap of paper inside. He had betrayed me! I was faithful, never taking my engagement ring off, giving up everything for the second time, and this is what he had been up to. I was destroyed. How could I have been so foolish? Jim tried to convince me of his innocence, other than being at the wrong place at the wrong time, and that might well have been. He said it was a teacher from a nearby town who hit on him when he was at a bar with his friends. She handed him her number, and that was the end of it. Obviously they had spoken long enough for him to know a few things about her, but how much?

After all of the inconsistencies, I didn't know what to believe, but one thing was for sure: I was devastated. All of my hopes came crashing down, and the suspicions and questions flooded back. At this time, two of our pastors asked me to go out to lunch with them. As we were eating, one said, "We feel like you are a candle, flickering, almost ready to be snuffed out." My eyes welled up with tears. Someone had recognized my thinly veiled pain. They prayed with me and tried to encourage me, but to no avail.

Jim and I continued to date for a few months, but it was turbulent, to say the least. Fighting for the relationship beyond what was reasonable, I didn't think I could reveal to another man what we had done together physically. No one else would want me. I was used material, impure and worthless. Beyond miserable, I finally decided to end my life. The despair and darkness were palpable. It was difficult to face another morning, and there was no joy, even on sunny spring days. I was wounded deeply, unable to care what it would do to Jim if he felt any responsibility for my death. I was a failure. People I met would say I looked familiar, but they couldn't place me. I wanted to scream, "I'm Laurie Holm, the runner!" Didn't anyone remember me? The girl with such high hopes was reduced to nothing. After contemplating suicide for quite some time, the pain absolutely became unbearable. It lasted around the clock, never retreating.

At that time, I believed I would go to hell if I took my own life, but I was already in hell now. Could it be any worse? I could not go on. Now all that was left was to decide how to do it. I considered shooting myself in the head, but I didn't want to make a mess at my parents' house. After all, this wasn't their fault. I thought I might take pills, but how many and what kind? I didn't want to increase my pain by becoming violently ill yet not accomplish the goal.

All of a sudden, I was gripped with the reality of what I was going to do. With the last bit of strength I had, I cried out to God, "Help me!" That is all I could utter since I had nothing left inside to carry on. Instantly I felt my whole being flooded with peace, a peace I'd never known before in my entire life. I also heard a voice repeat over and over in my head, "You *will* be happy again." It was not an audible voice, but it had all of the strength and comfort I desperately needed. Knowing it came from God, it was my life boat, what I would cling to in the lonely days to come, and it gave me courage.

I broke up with Jim for what I thought would be the last time in June of 1981. Something very strange happened later that summer. I had a dream about Jim, and he was at a house party. He had been drinking excessively and fell into the swimming pool and drowned. Then I saw him after death, but he had not made it to heaven. I woke up crying violently and felt an urgency to pray for Jim all day. Even though he would not be a part of my life, I sincerely did care for and want the best for him. It was the first time I wanted Jim to change for *his* sake rather than mine. Healing had finally begun. I was beginning to see outside of myself and my pain with increasing frequency.

I made the decision to go back to school in the fall, but this time at the University of Montana. I figured I had blown it too badly at Montana State to even attempt to go back. My scholarship was long gone, and I couldn't afford to live away from home and pay for school, too. I tried to focus on training and planned to be a walk-on for the cross country team. The coach welcomed me and even with my recent past, was willing to give me a chance on his team. It was a bit difficult competing against MSU in meets that fall because I had so many wonderful memories there. It seemed I should be warming up with them instead.

Cross country training camp was about to begin prior to the start of school when Jim called. It was so good to hear his voice. He wanted to talk, and I agreed to meet with him. We spent the evening at a park, and it was very comfortable. We had each dated other people during those summer months, but no one compared to Jim. I desperately wanted to be with my one and only true love. The romance with him was rekindled, and I left for training camp. Ten days later, we were married at his parents' house. We decided on a Monday at noon and were married Tuesday, September 22, 1981, at 7:00 p.m.

Wedding photo, September 1981.

Shortly after we were married, Jim told me he needed to run an errand. We were driving along together and stopped at an apartment I'd never been to before. He told me to wait for him in the truck, so I did. He returned with a backpack that belonged to a friend of his, so we drove toward the owner's house to drop it off. I asked him whose backpack it was and why he had it—an innocent enough question. With reservation, he explained that he had borrowed it from his friend so a girl he'd dated during the summer could use it. I pressured him for a little more information and found out they had gone backpacking together to a place called Heart Lake. When he stopped at her place, he also had to tell her he was married and wouldn't be calling anymore. She must have thought we were both a little bit crazy.

I understood he had dated others during that summer prior to our marriage and I had no legitimate claim on him. However, I was wounded by the fact that it appeared so easy for him to move on so quickly from our relationship when I was unable to. As much as I love the outdoors, he had never even taken me backpacking before. Suspicious about whether they'd slept together, other than being in the same tent, I pressed hard for more information. He angrily said no but he would have if she had allowed it. My heart ached. That was almost as bad as if they had been intimate, simply because he said he wanted to. Had I been so easy to replace? Not allowing this subject to die, I would bring it up numerous times. He told me he had only said that in anger to hurt me because he was tired of hearing about it. I was not sure which story was true, but one thing was certain: I *was* hurt. Either way, mission accomplished. As much as I've always enjoyed hiking and nature, I've never gone backpacking due to the memories it conjured up. This location also happened to be a favorite hiking destination for many of my family members, so each time they said they went to Heart Lake, mine broke just a little bit more.

My time running for UM was short-lived, as I only completed my first cross country season there. I quit because I felt I needed to stay home on weekends once I found out Jim was still going out with his friends in my absence. We had received quite a few gifts of cash when we got married. One day when I went to retrieve the envelope containing the money, it was nearly all gone. Jim had been using our wedding gift to fund his nights out at the bars with his friends. When my coach had volunteered to drop me off at home once after a cross country meet, he asked how my marriage was going. My response was, "Two months of torture." Not surprisingly, our early married life was equally as turbulent as our courtship. We had serious trust issues, as nothing had really changed. I gave up my dreams once again, naively assuming that being available to monitor Jim's activities would improve our relationship. However, my decision caused me to have great feelings of resentment toward him later on.

I am amazed at how hasty my decisions were during this period of time. It was so out of character for me to be so erratic, always having been so dependable and goal-oriented. To continually give up what I worked extremely hard for is difficult to fathom, but that is exactly what happened. I was miserable, and I'm sure Jim was too, but I kept remembering the promise from God that I would be happy again. Without that, I am positive I could not have survived.

CHAPTER 5

STEEP HILL

I will turn their mourning into gladness; I will give them
comfort and joy instead of sorrow.
                                        —Jeremiah 31:13b

One part of this illness involves blaming others for your unhappiness. I blamed Jim for the fact I quit running. I could make a pretty convincing argument for that, but the truth of the matter is, I am the one who ultimately made the choice. I have no one to blame but myself and possibly the distorted thinking of this crazy illness. In addition to blaming my husband, I also blamed my parents for being too fair with me as a child. I believed they had not prepared me for the injustices in life. Have you ever heard of an adult daughter accusing her parents of being too good to her? I also blamed my sister, to a small degree, for giving me advice about whether to have sex with Jim before we were married. If that hadn't happened, I thought maybe I wouldn't have fought so hard to save the dysfunctional relationship. I had given Jim my most precious gift, which I was saving solely for the man I would marry. Mostly, I blamed myself for being so stupid as I floundered along in life. I could not seem to keep my life on course no matter what I did. The truth of the matter is that I didn't have a full understanding of what grace is. If I had been able to forgive myself, I may have been able to refrain from blaming others for my own decisions.

Now that I understand more about my husband and have seen him change over the years, I am able to trust him deeply. In our early years, he would do anything in order to avoid conflict. Oftentimes there wasn't anything worth hiding, but it was his way of dealing with things. Unfortunately, instead of inhibiting conflict, it actually created more. As we walked through the difficulties of our first years together as husband and wife, we were both miserable. I was frequently extremely depressed, though never suicidal. I kept those words "You will be happy again" tucked away in my heart, longing for the day when it would finally happen.

Sometimes I wondered what it would have been like to be married to other men. Surely they treated their wives better than Jim treated me. It seemed like other couples were much happier. Out of frustration early on in our marriage, I packed a suitcase and asked Jim to drop me off at my mom and dad's house. Like a gentleman, he waited in the truck to make sure they were home. My mom came to the door, looked at my suitcase, and asked me what I was doing. Sensing her disapproval, I said in embarrassment, "I thought I'd stay here a little while." Her response startled me. I had made my choice and needed to live with it. Mom seemed a bit angry, and I felt like such a disappointment. Her reaction was not what I expected, but it was the best gift she could have given us. There was nowhere for me to run away from my problems, because my sister had recently moved to Wyoming and I honestly couldn't think of another option.

I became pregnant with our first son the next spring. We were poor and barely had food to eat. I was concerned about whether the baby would be healthy because I did not gain any weight during the first six months of pregnancy. Too proud to tell anyone about our situation, we "happened" to stop by our parents' houses around the dinner hour and hoped they would invite us to eat. Jim's folks had purchased a huge case of hot dogs from a friend who worked at a packaging plant, so that's what they often were having when we'd come. For the most part I did not struggle with morning sickness. The only food that turned my stomach were hotdogs, but I managed to choke them down somehow, out of necessity. Just to set the record straight, Jim's mom was a fabulous cook. It was just poor timing.

I finally talked Jim into letting me go to a WIC (Women, Infants, and Children) meeting, where I could get vouchers for food. He hated the idea, and I have to admit, it was a very humbling experience. At the meeting, I filled out a form showing what I'd eaten that day. The directions stated to list items separately—for example, if you had milk on your cereal. I followed the instructions and completed the form. A caseworker then sat down with me and started marking up my paper as she asked questions. "So you had cereal and drank a half cup of milk?"

"No, I put that milk on my cereal."

She seemed confused as she kept crossing out and adding things. Apparently she had not expected me to follow the directions. I was also shown rubber food to help me understand what a half cup of green beans looked like, for example. The next thing I had to do was go to the grocery store and actually redeem the vouchers, another humbling experience with no husband beside me to support me. After those experiences and with Jim so opposed to it, I could not go back. I decided to pray for a healthy baby.

At Christmastime that year, though we did not have money to buy each other presents, we were automatically included in drawing names in Jim's family to purchase gifts for his siblings and their spouses. They also set a price range for these gifts. I wasn't sure by what means we were going to be able to participate, but how does one admit to people that you cannot afford to join in? I lamented to my husband about this predicament yet set out to try to accomplish the impossible. Amazingly, I was able to find nice gifts at a huge savings. I decided no one would know I hadn't spent the appropriate sum, since the regular price of each item fell within that range. I came home from shopping, proudly showing Jim what wonderful deals I had found. The items were then stacked on the coffee table. I was feeling starved, so I fixed a sandwich and a tall glass of milk. With satisfaction, I returned to the coffee table, accidentally spilling the milk right next to the gifts. Fearing they would be ruined, I let out an expletive, and Jim laughed at me, startled since I never used words like that. Instantly, I grabbed my sandwich, stood up, and threw it about fifteen feet, hitting Jim square in the face. I then stormed off to the bedroom, not even wiping up the mess on the table. A little bit later, after cleaning up my mess, Jim walked in sheepishly, holding a new glass of milk and a plate with a sandwich on it. As he came slowly toward me with this peace offering, I began to laugh since he still had mayonnaise where the sandwich had hit him on the face! In such a short period of time, I had gone from being so proud of what I had accomplished, to rage, to laughter. Hormones from pregnancy or bipolar disorder? Maybe a little bit of both.

Our son, Garrett James Johnson, was born on February 16, 1983. After all of my nutritional concerns, and being induced early, he was a whopping ten-pound, twelve-ounce boy and twenty-two inches long. He even had little rolls of fat. As an infant, Jim had been overdue by three weeks, and at fourteen pounds, six ounces, and twenty-six inches long, was the second biggest baby ever born in North Dakota. Somewhere in the recesses of my mind, I was concerned about having a large baby like Jim. Dreams can bring out funny things people worry about. I had one dream while pregnant where Garrett was so big when he was born, he jumped down off the table and said, "Hi, Mom!" I guess I actually got off pretty easy after all.

Since we did not have insurance at the time, I came home from the hospital a little earlier than I probably should have. When I entered the front door of our mobile home, my entire living room was filled with Jim's family! He hadn't told me they were coming over because they wanted to surprise me. Oh, it was a surprise, all right! I sat down in my rocking chair, holding the baby, and didn't even take my coat off. I was a bit unsure how to react because I just wanted to go to bed. Then Jim's mom said, "How's my little Chip doing?" Okay, that was it! She had been saying during my pregnancy that if I had a boy, she was going to call him Chip. My feeling was that she'd had nine children, and if she wanted to name anyone Chip, she should have named one of her own children that! After all, this was my first and maybe only child, and I was going to name him what I wanted. I begged Jim to talk to her about it before he was born, but he obviously hadn't. I may have just been tired enough or hormonal enough, but whatever it was, I replied instantly and very firmly, "His name is Garrett." I still cannot believe I had the guts to say that to my mother-in-law. I am actually glad it happened the way it did, because under normal circumstances, I probably would have just let her continue to call him whatever she wanted, begrudging her for it the entire time. Garrett is very thankful that he is not Chip, by the way!

Jim previously said he did not want children, and then when I became pregnant he said, "Just one boy." After Garrett was born, Jim was so proud he stated he wanted three or four more boys. There was no doubt about it, Garrett was a blessing. During the rough times when

I contemplated leaving Jim, I thought about Garrett getting tossed back and forth between us, and I hung in there. I was attempting to finish my education degree at UM, but at a snail's pace. I would take a class or two at a time and was in and out of school so much, it seemed I would never graduate. Occasionally I had to take Garrett to school with me, which was less than pleasant. I found it hard to concentrate, as I imagine it was for others in the class as well.

Jim and I were very involved in our church. Though embarrassed at being unable to afford nice outfits for church, I continued to attend anyway. I kept my old leather shoes in repair by sewing the seams together every so often, but the soles became so thin I could feel the rocks jab my feet from underneath. I had joined his church when we were dating and thoroughly loved it. The people were wonderful, and we had a very active Young Marrieds group. We attended classes, shared food at each others' homes, and had retreats up at a Bible camp. This was a lifeline for me at an extremely difficult time in my life.

Jim's sister and her husband were also involved in the Young Marrieds. She was a little older than Jim and married longer, but they had no children yet. His sister and I got pregnant about the same time; it would be my second child and her first. We were excited to go through pregnancy together until she received some bad news. Her baby was not going to survive. I cannot remember exactly what was wrong, but I do recollect feeling terrible as I grew larger and she did not. After enjoying the prospect of this shared experience, now there was guilt since I would have two children and she would have none. I hesitated whenever I knew I would be seeing her for fear it would rub salt into the wound.

When I found out I was pregnant for the second time, I was in school and on the insurance plan. After having to pay all of the expenses for Garrett's birth, it seemed like a good idea to maintain insurance coverage by taking at least one class each quarter until the baby was born. God had looked out for us in many ways during my first pregnancy, but it seemed unwise to take any chances. Garrett was actually breach up until six weeks prior to delivery. My physician was the only one in Missoula who could turn a baby before delivery. The doctor must push on the behind and on the face of the baby externally. It required quite a lot of effort, as one can imagine, and was not a pleasant experience.

This procedure was performed at that stage of the pregnancy because the baby will not usually turn again. Also, if the umbilical cord somehow got wrapped around the neck, it is possible to have a good outcome if the baby needed to be delivered quickly. Due to Garrett's size, if he had remained breach, it most certainly would have resulted in a Caesarian section, which is much more expensive than delivering naturally. Thankfully the procedure to turn him was successful and did not result in an emergency birth.

While pregnant with my second child, in addition to school, I obtained work as a grocery store sampler for a beverage company. Since we had so little money, this would help with the bills somewhat. The job allowed for a very flexible schedule so I could work around Jim's commitments, which was important, since paying for daycare was a huge consideration. One day a man approached me at my stand and said, "Aren't you that great runner?" in a sarcastic tone. I recognized him but didn't even know his name at that time. He continued and asked, "Why are you sampling pop? We expected so much more from you than this." It was another in a series of messages about my failures that dealt me a blow. I had no answer for him.

Though not running, I maintained a fair amount of fitness during my pregnancies. We went hiking up a fairly steep trail on Mount Sentinel while I was pregnant, and I carried Garrett on my back in a child carrier. The friends we were hiking with were surprised I would even attempt such a climb. During my first pregnancy with Garrett, I remember riding my bike until I couldn't pedal up a small hill since my belly was in the way. With my knees sticking out to the sides, I couldn't seem to produce the force necessary to pedal, so I turned around mid-hill and put the bike away until after he was born.

Brent Andrew Johnson was born on November 16, 1984, exactly one year and nine months after Garrett. His name meant "steep hill," which I was not too excited about, but I loved the name anyway. I did not want him to have a hard time in life, but that's what it made me think of. Though I didn't care whether I had a boy or girl, I thought he might actually be a sweet little girl, since the pregnancy was so much different than with his brother. Garrett was a handful—very clever, always into mischief. When I was pregnant with him, it hurt under my ribs because he kicked so hard. Brent, on the other hand, was so still some days I wondered if the baby was even alive. Then I would feel a soft little movement and my mind would rest at ease. Children are just different, right?

Garrett loved his little brother but didn't understand that when you played football with Brent, the baby is not the football. I had to watch him closely, which was nothing new. When I brought Garrett to a portrait studio, a friend of mine took the pictures of him. When we returned to get them, she said she hadn't realized how cute he was because she usually only saw him from the back as he was running away. Another time I was going crazy with fear because I couldn't find Garrett in a large store. After a frenzied search, I was about to ask them to lock down the store in case he was abducted. Then I heard a little giggle from inside a circular clothing rack. Sure enough, there he was, hiding from me. My life became quite busy as I took care of a boisterous toddler and a newborn.

At Brent's three-month well-check, his doctor noticed he was not moving as much as one would expect for his age. Brent was growing to be a big boy, so the doctor said it might be that he was simply a very happy, laid-back sort. He told me to watch for movement in the coming weeks and months, but it was probably nothing. The doctor also told me to put him in the bathtub a lot so it would be easier for such a big baby to move since he would be buoyant. Brent was the most content baby I'd known, and after how active Garrett was, I thought it might be a blessing. Brent's life did turn out to be a blessing, but not in the way one might think.

When we were at my parents' house for Easter, Brent was about five months old. My mom hadn't seen the kids in awhile, so she immediately picked Brent up off the blanket on the floor. As she did so, I tried to warn her to support his head, but it was too late. She expected him to have better strength than he did, so he banged his face on her collar bone. My always happy baby cried miserably. Mom felt terrible, but that's what caused me to realize something was dreadfully wrong with my son. My mom, who raised six children, would know what a child that age was supposed to be doing. I really should have known as well, but when you are with someone every day, it is harder to recognize he is gradually deteriorating, especially when you may be in denial. The simple fact that I attempted to warn her also showed me that deep down I knew something was wrong. I made a doctor's appointment immediately, and the testing began.

Jim was a great dad in many ways but not terribly interested in changing diapers or bathing kids. Since I nursed my babies, he did not get up in the night either, but I loved everything about being a mother, so that was not a huge problem. I took care of the basic needs and played with the children, and Dad just played! Once the myriad of doctor's appointments began, however, I was left on my own to handle it, and Jim quit paying attention to Brent. I couldn't figure out what the problem was but would try to get Jim involved by placing the baby in his arms for a picture or ask him to entertain Brent while I was busy doing something else that needed my attention. It became frustrating to me because I felt I was managing everything alone, and I needed some support.

As things progressed, Brent had a hard time sleeping for more than an hour at a time. From the time of his birth, he couldn't even turn his head from one side to the other while on his tummy. I was hardly sleeping since I would turn him and massage him during the night, just imagining his discomfort. Daytime was difficult too, because I was obsessive about keeping my house clean, playing with Garrett, who was jealous at times, and attending to Brent. My poor little baby should have been able to entertain himself but would just lay there looking at the ceiling. Guilt-ridden and trying to be super-mom, I would hurriedly finish up the dishes or whatever else I was doing so I could play with him. He couldn't even hold a small rattle for more than a second or two but was cognitively completely normal, trapped inside his nearly paralyzed body.

Brent at about six months of age, May 1985.
It is easy to see his weight gain from being immobile.

Brent and Garrett, ready for bed.

Brent and Garrett, best buddies.

I took Brent to all of his appointments by myself, giving Jim the report as one thing after another was ruled out. The doctors knew of only one more possibility. Testing for it involved a muscle biopsy, removal of tissue from his right thigh, which was sent to Washington DC to be analyzed. We received the results in late June of 1985. Brent had Spinal Muscular Atrophy, otherwise known as Werdnig-Hoffman disease. It is a neuro-muscular disease where the brain is fine and the muscles are fine, but the anterior horn cells in the spine are defective. The brain sends a message to the muscles. However, the message gets lost, and the muscles atrophy from lack of use. When people with this genetic disorder catch a cold, they become susceptible to pneumonia since they are too weak to clear the secretions. The cause of death is actually pneumonia due to Werdnig-Hoffman disease. It is always fatal.

Brent needed to see a pediatric neurologist who, despite his good intentions, actually added to the stress I was under. He told me of a thirty-year-old patient who became a painter, using his mouth to hold the brush. The doctor was trying to give me a dose of hope, but it backfired. Already feeling overwhelmed by my daily responsibilities, I envisioned assisting someone my husband's size in the future. This would involve bathing, lifting, feeding, and meeting all my son's other needs for years, perhaps decades. At age twenty-four, this seemed like a life sentence. Then the guilt began. I loved my son dearly and wanted him to live but didn't know how I would cope, especially with a distant, disengaged husband.

At a subsequent visit, as the burden weighed heavily upon me, I asked the specialist, "I know what you told me about your former patient, but how long do you think *my* son will live?" He stated that there is more than one form of this disease, depending upon age of onset. "Children like Brent usually succumb within the first year or two of their lives." Now I understood time was short and I needed to focus on making every moment count. Part of my huge burden was lifted, and the guilt was gone.

One particular Sunday morning before church, I had fed and bathed the boys but still needed to get myself ready. Jim was in bed, so I brought Brent to him. I laid him beside Jim and in a pleading voice said, *"Please play with him."* He assured me he would. After showering, I returned to our room and found Brent staring at the ceiling while his dad slept. I woke Jim and all I could say was, "You are going to be so sorry." Unfortunately, nothing changed.

In late July, my sister, who had never seen Brent, came from Wyoming to visit. She felt an urgent need to be with me, so she packed up all four of her young children and drove to Missoula. We had a wonderful time together, taking the kids swimming and visiting with family. The day after she left and Jim had gone to work in the evening, Brent grew very restless. When I tried to nurse him, he couldn't, which was unusual since he always liked to eat. Garrett was already in bed, and I had dim lighting in the living room as I tried to get Brent to go to sleep. I turned up the dimmer switch to get a good look at Brent, since his pediatrician told me I should take him to the hospital if his lips began turning blue. I hadn't even realized Brent was coming down with anything, but there it was, a bluish tinge around his lips. I called Jim and told him to meet me at the hospital, asked the neighbor to come over and stay with Garrett, held Brent up close to my chest, and prayed. Then off we went.

Brent's photos, taken at eight months of age, were ready just in time for the memorial service. They gave us the entire package at no cost when they found out he had died on August 5, 1985.

After arriving at the hospital, it was necessary to explain to the nurses what was wrong and the proposed treatment plan. There was not a single nurse who had even heard of Werdnig-Hoffman disease because so little was known about it at the time. They followed my instructions until the doctor arrived.

The next four days were spent by Brent's side after we made the decision to keep him as comfortable as possible rather than fight to keep him alive. We couldn't bear the thought of him suffering through pneumonia a second time. Heaven is a better option than that. During those four days and nights, I still held out hope that God could heal him of this disease. With optimism in my voice, I told my mom one night that his name meant "steep hill," but there is always a top to every hill. My mom left the room, probably in anguish over watching her grandson and her own baby hurting. She did not want to see me disappointed in the outcome. I needed a dose of reality at that point, so once again my mom brought me back without saying a word.

I do know that God can heal people miraculously, but we can't force God's hand. It has to be His will, His plan, and for His purpose. I think the greatest miracles are when people rise in the face of adversity with hope and faith intact, trusting God knows best. In this case, His will was to take my son far too early for my liking, but I've never felt closer to God than at that time.

While at the hospital, I had what I would call a vision. Some might call it a hallucination, but I prefer to say vision since, rather than causing me to be fearful, it was a tremendous comfort to me. About two days before Brent died, as I was holding my baby's hand and rubbing his arm, I saw Jesus in the room. He picked up Brent and carried him away slowly. As they moved away, I noticed Jesus was not supporting Brent's back and head like I always had to. Then Brent turned to look at me and gave me that big smile of his. It made it easier to let him go, knowing he was safe in the arms of Jesus and he would be whole, not trapped in a prison for a body.

During the final night prior to his death, Brent woke up. I had just gone to the next room to lay down, but hadn't fallen asleep. The nurses felt sorry for me since I hadn't gotten much rest in several days, so they told me I could lay on the bed as long as I didn't pull down the covers. Someone ran to get me just moments after I left to inform me that Brent was awake, so I hurried in to see him. As soon as he recognized me, he tried to cry. It was as if he was pleading, "Mommy, help me, I hurt so bad. Make it all better!" Since Brent had pneumonia, he could not make a sound, but the look of panic said it all. I caressed him but couldn't make this go away. He only seemed to become more upset. My heart was breaking because I had always been able to fix anything. Mommy was helpless. I thought maybe if he couldn't see me, he would settle down. Breathing was already much too difficult without him being upset. I left the room. That was the last time my son ever saw me, and I had abandoned him. It took a while to forgive myself, but I know I left the room with the best of intentions. We humans have a way of making ourselves feel guilty when dealing with grief, even when it isn't warranted.

Throughout the time we spent in the hospital, friends and family came and went as they offered us support. The nursing staff and our pediatrician were excellent as well. People took care of Garrett for us and brought meals to us.

On August 5, 1985, around 7:00 p.m., when Brent's time on this earth was almost over, a nurse told me I should hold him. I hadn't tried to pick him up since I'd found it frustrating on the first day in the hospital. He was connected to an IV, oxygen, and a heart rate monitor, not to mention it had also become increasingly difficult under normal circumstances to properly support his growing body. I wanted to hold him up to my chest with his head on my shoulder like I normally did, but that was impossible. When the nurse suggested I hold him, it was in such a way I did not even remotely question it, though it did take me off guard. Apparently she was seeing signs the end was nearing, but I had been oblivious to it.

This nurse gave me such a gift by alerting me. I took him in my arms. As I held him, all of a sudden I felt him leave. A difficult thing to explain, it was similar to a complete and total relaxing of whatever muscles he did have any use of. I could also tell his spirit was not in his body any longer. I cannot describe it; it is just something I know. I gazed up from Brent after saying, "He's gone. He's dead," and noticed people were looking at me, puzzled. I then glanced at the monitor, which showed he still had a heartbeat. His pulse was slowing, and eventually he flat-lined, but as I sat there waiting for it to happen, I was feeling a strange sort of disconnect with Brent's body. I was holding an empty shell! That was no longer my son, and I knew it. To me this was proof that the body and spirit are two totally separate entities. It also made it easier for me to part with Brent's body at the hospital.

Jim had a very hard time letting go. After Brent's body was held by many friends and family members as they said their good-byes, it was laid back on his little hospital bed. Everyone left us to be alone in the room with Brent after singing, "Jesus Loves Me." Jim stood there touching his body and said to me "I thought if I didn't get close to him, it wouldn't hurt as much, but I was wrong." This was the first time I ever saw my husband cry. I felt a sense of compassion and understanding for Jim that melted away any resentment from not having the support I desired in the past months. I was actually the more fortunate one because I hadn't missed out on knowing Brent.

We had investigated the possibility of donating Brent's organs so other people wouldn't have to experience the loss of their child as we had. That was not to be. Since there was so little information about this disease, it was unknown if it would be passed to the organ recipient. The only thing we were allowed to donate were his corneas. We later received a letter from the Montana Eye Bank telling of two little girls who could see. One was a six-month-old who was born blind, the other a three-year-old who lost her sight in an accident. As nice as that was, it would have been wonderful to be able to help even more children. Some day I would like to meet those girls.

A few days later, a memorial service was held for Brent, where Jim and I actually shared about him. We had a private family time at the cemetery earlier in the day for internment of his tiny little white casket. Somehow I had so much strength and peace throughout this time. I was even consoling other people. Jim and I were also getting along better than we ever had. It is amazing what the Lord can help you through when you lean on Him.

I decided to box up Brent's clothes and put away the crib shortly thereafter. I shed a few tears, but it was not as bad as one might expect. When my loss really hit me was in the day-to-day things. His crib had been in our tiny bedroom, so I always had to turn sideways to get between it and our king-sized waterbed. That was no longer necessary. It was a reminder that he was really gone. At the park in the fall, I pushed down on the empty end of a teeter totter so Garrett could have a ride. I should have been steadying a healthy Brent on that end. Friends who hadn't seen me in a while asked me how many kids I had. They were later mortified for bringing it up if I told them I had two, but one passed away. It's hard to pretend your child never existed, and I wanted to talk about him. Sometimes telling just wasn't worth dealing with the discomfort it caused others. Most of my grieving happened when I was at home in the evening after Jim left for work and Garrett had gone to bed. I would pull out Brent's photo album and cry. These times became increasingly spread apart, causing less anguish and fewer tears along the way.

A few months later, when Brent would have been turning one, I spent his birthday at home with Garrett. It was a lonely day of housework, but I tried to convince myself that's what I would have been doing anyway in preparation for his party. I wished someone would remember me on this difficult day, but the phone did not ring once. I didn't call anyone either because I felt it would be awkward to phone someone just to bring it up. Not to mention, I guess I really wanted someone to think of it on their own and reach out to me, so I grieved silently. Finally, at 5:00 p.m., there was a knock on the door, but I wasn't expecting anyone. When I opened the door, a man was standing there with a nice bouquet of flowers. After he left, I read the card, and it said, "Thinking of you today. Love, Your Secret Pal." Someone had remembered me in a quiet, painful moment. It brought tears to my eyes. I wouldn't find out who my secret pal was until almost a year later, when we chose new ones at church. It turned out to be a friend of mine whose sister had died of cancer. When I finally was able to thank her for such a thoughtful gift, she told me she understood how important it was to acknowledge the first birthday without him because of what she and her family had undergone.

I learned some very important lessons from the painful experience of losing a precious child. First, we should never feel guilty for our blessings because we do not know what the next day may hold. I learned this because of how I felt about being able to have a second child when my sister-in-law lost her first one. Then Brent died in my arms. We need to have compassion for others when they are experiencing difficult times, but it is okay to still appreciate our own blessings.

The second lesson is to refrain from being hard on ourselves or each other when we are doing the best we can to handle the worst possible thing life can throw at us. I learned this partly because of when I left the room when Brent woke up. After all, I had good intentions and could not bear it if my presence was causing him to struggle even more. People also handle tragic circumstances differently from each other. I function better if I know what I am dealing with, while at this time Jim felt if he ignored it, there would be less pain. Treating others with understanding is always better than judgment when dealing with grief.

The most important lesson I learned is that walking through life without the Lord at my side would make it unbearable. I don't know how I would have been able to handle the loss of my son without Him.

Brent's marker at his grave.

CHAPTER 6

FAITH

Now faith is being sure of what we hope for and certain of what we do not see.

—Hebrews 11 :1

Once we found out what was wrong with Brent and were told it is always fatal, I prayed for his healing. After all, who wouldn't? I thought if I just believed hard enough, he would be healed. I believed, yet he still died. Somehow, miraculously, it did not shake my faith. I know of others who have become very disillusioned when they prayed, believed, and then didn't get what they were asking for.

God wants to give us good gifts. The key is to pray according to God's will. The question is, how do we know what God's will is? I believe God wants us to ask for what we want, making sure our motives are pure and ultimately trusting He knows best. The best analogy I can describe is to compare the parent/child relationship to the heavenly Father/human relationship. If a child asks for a toy or candy, sometimes it is given to him right away, sometimes he must wait for it (like saving candy until after a meal or a toy for a special occasion), and other times the parent doesn't buy it at all because the budget is too tight, the child already has enough, or it's bad for him. Simply by requesting, a child probably receives more than if he never asked for anything. It would not be to his benefit if he were given everything he asked for, however, because the child would grow up expecting everything and not appreciating anything. In other words, as the parent, you know best. We love to give our children treats but know it would be detrimental to treat them to everything. It is in the disappointments and hardships where we grow the most.

Does saying no to our children mean we love them any less? Of course not; it actually can mean we love them more. It's easy to crumble and say yes, even when it is something we don't feel completely at peace about. That is human nature. Thankfully, God's nature is perfect, and as much as it must hurt Him to see us in pain, He knows exactly what we need in order to be mature and complete, which means we will face trials in this life. I have come to love the book of James in the New Testament, especially chapter 1, which communicates this: "Consider it pure joy, my brothers, whenever you face trials of many kinds, because you know that the testing of your faith develops perseverance. Perseverance must finish its work so that you may be mature and complete, not lacking anything" (James 1:2–4).

After losing Brent, I desperately wanted to fill my empty mother's arms. I missed carrying the diaper bag around, I missed my precious alone time with him in the night, and I missed Brent. I always wanted to have several children, but the genetic counselor informed us that we should not have any more children due to the one in four chance that this could happen to any child of ours. Having an only child was unfathomable, so we went to adoption meetings. Even as a young child, I had it in my heart to adopt children, so I thought maybe this would be how God wanted us to build our family.

We were still in a very poor state financially and found that even though some of the organizations had a sliding adoption fee, it was still completely unrealistic for us to be able to adopt. We listened to a woman speak at one meeting about her experiences and that her little daughter had a genetic disorder. When they adopted her, there was no indication of anything wrong. As she grew older they realized, though they were not life threatening, their daughter had health issues that would plague her for the rest of her life. We went home from the meeting with a lot to think about—mainly, that in life there are no guarantees.

Some of our friends had infertility problems. One couple we knew couldn't seem to get pregnant. Another couple was able to conceive but would later miscarry the baby. In our case, practically if we shook hands, I was pregnant! Conceiving and carrying to term were not an issue for us, but lack of money was. It seemed to me after listening to the woman at the adoption meeting that no matter how you expanded your family, it involved faith that God was in control. We could end up with a healthy child or a sick child no matter how he came to us. Could we trust God enough to take the chance of losing another child? Would it be right to play Russian Roulette with a baby's life? These are very difficult questions, and the answers will not be the same for everyone.

Desperate for a baby, we prayed. We prayed God would give us a baby naturally. Then I specifically asked Him for a healthy baby, and if the child wouldn't be healthy to please not allow me to conceive. I went on and said, "But if You choose to give us another child and that child has the same disease, I will trust You." After all, I felt that Brent had been perfectly planned for us. His life had value and meaning, even though he died at just under nine months of age. We grew so much individually and as a couple through having him, so I believed God knew best. He was trustworthy.

After sufficiently praying together about having another child, I conceived right away. I went through the pregnancy totally at peace. We had never actually prayed about having a child before; we simply had them. Not everyone had an identical reaction to my pregnancy, however. One person said, "How could you *do* this to us!" I have to say, I was a bit irritated about it at the time, since I'm the one who held my own son as he died. I don't think this individual really had any idea what I had just gone through. I ultimately chalked it up to two things. First, she was entitled to her own feelings about it, which were not for me to judge. Second, sometimes feelings are best kept to oneself.

My mom's only words in response to the news of the impending birth were, "Oh, Laurie." That's it. I was not angry in the least, because I completely understood her response. She had watched her precious grandson suffer, and she had watched her precious daughter suffer. Her reaction was totally natural. Mom has an uncanny way of saying a lot when she's not saying a lot, which you may have already guessed from reading this far into my story. One thing I have always appreciated about my mom is that she knows it will do no good to express her opinions when a decision has already been made—though she is happy to give advice when asked!

Our pediatrician's reaction was the most surprising. When I took Garrett to his next well check, with some apprehension I told Dr. Hardy I was pregnant and it was planned. He was excited for us! I did not expect that reaction from someone in the medical field at all. I also had some friends express their congratulations to us, though later they admitted their concern. Of one thing I was confident: people were praying for all of us. It was nice to have friends and family members congratulate us on our new little bundle who would be arriving in October of 1986.

I regularly felt the baby kick during this pregnancy. It wasn't as strong as with my first son, but I never experienced days where I might have wondered if the baby was alive. No matter how inconclusive that was, I did not worry at all, which is a miracle in itself. Then the day finally arrived. I say finally, because my dear friend Patty and I were both due on October 9, and she had her daughter in September. From the time her daughter, Kristen, was born, everyone would say, "Are you still around?" At the end of a pregnancy, that is the last thing I wanted to hear, especially when I wasn't even due yet. My beautiful son Chad Michael Johnson was born a couple of weeks after Kristen but six days early on October 3, 1986.

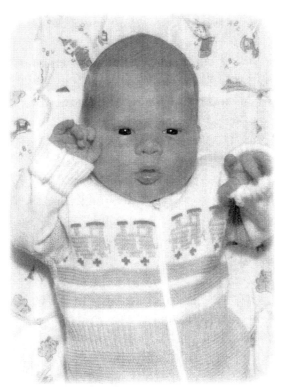

Chad's newborn hospital picture.

Garrett, happy to meet his new little brother Chad, October 1986.

Chad was a full pound smaller than Garrett as a newborn, but at nine pounds, twelve ounces, he was not tiny by any means. He was extremely cute and greatly resembled Brent, so much so that Jim mistakenly called him Brent on many occasions. I didn't really care whether I had a boy or a girl but thought it was a nice gift since we might be getting a glimpse of what Brent could have looked like at various ages as Chad grew. Though it may sound otherwise, I never viewed Chad as a replacement for Brent. He was such a wonderful blessing, and I'm so glad we decided to have him.

I'd like to say I chose Chad's name because of its meaning, but that's not entirely the case. My husband was unaware at the time, but I liked the name because I remembered a cute blond-haired boy from Bible camp when I was in grade school whose name was Chad. That boy didn't even know I existed, though. Garrett's name means spear-brave, and Chad's name means warlike. It's probably not wise to name two children in the same home with warrior-type names, but after what we had gone through with Brent, a good, strong name was appealing!

The only way to know if Chad had Werdnig-Hoffman disease was to do a muscle biopsy or to be patient and wait to see if he moved as he should at different ages. Remembering how Brent had cried from the procedure and how big the scar looked on his little thigh, I decided I would rather not put Chad through that. We had waited nine months already; what difference would a few more make? After a sufficient period of time passed, we saw Chad doing the things babies do, albeit a bit later than his brother. Garrett walked at ten months and Chad at thirteen months, for example. But there was no mistaking it, Chad was healthy! God had given me my first choice when he answered my prayer. I felt so blessed. A woman at church said to me, "You always knew he would be all right." I really didn't, but I knew we would be all right because God would see us through anything. "In you I trust, O my God" (Ps. 25:2a).

I was twenty-five years old when Chad was born. Within a little over three and a half years, I had given birth to two sons, one son died, and then I had a third son. That is a lot to adjust to in a short period of time, especially considering my age and the turbulent start to our marriage. I thought having Chad would satisfy my desire for anymore babies, no matter what the outcome, so I stayed in the hospital a little longer after his birth to have a tubal ligation procedure. Our family would be complete. After Chad turned one, I found I still desired to have more children. Had I made a dreadful mistake deciding on this surgery at such a young age? That is a question I would ask myself many times in the coming years.

Chad gave us a couple of scares early in his life. We were on a camping trip the summer before he turned three when he had a seizure as he and I walked along a trail from the bathroom to our campsite. We had just finished brushing our teeth before starting the evening campfire. The next thing I knew, he was on the ground and his lips turned blue. Since he resembled his brother so much, it sent me quickly back to memories of the hospital when Brent was not getting enough oxygen. There was another little boy who had been admitted with Brent because he'd had a seizure, and initially they shared a room. This precious boy seized due to a brain tumor, which later claimed his life. Through my experience,

I only knew of two reasons people had seizures, and neither were good. It had to be epilepsy or a brain tumor, in my estimation.

Not knowing what else to do, we all got in the car, including the dog, and raced to the nearest town. On the way there, Garrett, only six at the time, said, "If he dies, I'll kill myself." I guess we'd underestimated the effect losing Brent had on Garrett at such a young age. Already concerned that my youngest son may have a potentially life-threatening condition, I tried to console his worried big brother.

We found a payphone and dialed 911. The Life Flight helicopter landed in a grade school playground, interrupting a softball game, to take Chad to a Missoula hospital. Since he was so young, the medical personnel wanted one of us to fly with him, so I did. This was not exactly how I'd dreamed of having my first helicopter ride, but there was no way my baby was going anywhere without me. Jim hurriedly packed up our campsite, stuffing things in the car every which way, and drove the hourlong trip back to town.

Chad was given oxygen on the way to the hospital, and by the time we were approaching Missoula, he was already quite alert. I began to feel like I'd overreacted when he looked out the window of the helicopter and said, "There's the M." We were flying at the same height as the university's giant concrete emblem on the mountain. As the emergency room doctor was checking on him, I was doing my best to describe what I had observed in Chad, all the while wondering if they believed me since he appeared to be fine. The diagnosis was a febrile seizure, due to a simple ear infection. It is caused when a person has a fever spike. It is common in little ones since their tiny bodies cannot handle the drastic change in body temperature that can occur in childhood illnesses. I hadn't even realized he was getting sick because he had played in the lake that day and acted normally until the moment the seizure began.

I began to wonder if we would have an annual panic with Chad, since the next summer when he was going on four years of age, he nearly had his hand crushed by a garage door. I was visiting my parents with the kids when Chad ran out the front door of their house with such purpose, it seemed he had a mission. I knew my dad was out in the front yard in their quiet neighborhood, so I didn't jump as quickly as I normally would.

When I heard my dad let out an alarming yell, I ran, with Mom following after. Dad was trying to hold the garage door up by his shoulder, and Chad's little hand was pinned between the door and the bracket holding the track for the wheels. This was an older door and didn't have the safety mechanism to cause it to go back up in this instance. Apparently Chad had run into the garage and grabbed the track for the garage door with his right hand and crossed over with his left hand to hit the button on the wall before my dad could react. At such a young age, Chad didn't know enough to hit it again to stop it.

I immediately pressed the button twice when I arrived—once to stop the downward motion, the second time to release Chad's hand by sending the door back up. My mom and I drove Chad quickly to the hospital, holding his hand up in a towel, while my dad dropped on the ground to his hands and knees. He doesn't do well with blood. After x-rays, we found out Chad had not broken any bones but needed stitches both inside and out. He still has a pretty nice scar between his thumb and first finger that goes partway across his hand. It really is a miracle there was not more damage, as he could have easily lost his hand. Not only did God give us our miracle baby, but he also kept him safe for us, and the annual catastrophes ended that year. Dad also updated his automatic garage door opener after this incident.

Chad's run-in with Grandpa's garage door at age 3, summer of 1989.

Chad and Garrett dressed up for our church Christmas program.

As a little guy, Chad was extremely fussy about what he wanted to wear. I've never known a three—or four-year-old boy who absolutely had to match, and his favorite color was bright orange. He had a preference for certain outfits, which made it difficult sometimes if I hadn't done laundry soon enough. He also liked to have his toys neatly displayed, which has carried over into his adult life. All of his DVDs and video games are in alphabetical order on the shelves. I'm pretty sure he gets this from me, since his dad was guilty of putting orange peels in a potted plant once early in our marriage. Jim told me later he was going to come back and get them but forgot! The perfectionist I was, I worried whether we'd had any company over who may have seen the orange peels before I noticed them.

The summer before Chad turned four, just prior to the garage door incident, we were at the park throwing some pitches to Garrett to help him get ready for baseball. Chad decided he wanted to try, but we didn't have any bats light enough for him to swing. Rather than say no and disappoint him, we let him attempt to hit the ball anyway, without success. I told him to choke up on the bat, and he gave me the most puzzled look. After sort of shrugging his shoulders, he turned his face to the bat and coughed out loud at it a few times. I actually fell on the ground laughing because he had taken it so literally. Little kids are so cute and trusting. It obviously didn't make sense to him, but I had told him to do it, so he figured, why not? That is the kind of childlike faith I desire to have. Even when I can't see the big picture, trust God anyway.

Chad always kept us laughing and was sort of a clown, especially during junior high. When we had our good friends and their little daughter over for a visit, he kept interrupting us, so I told him to go find something to do. Next thing we knew, he returned to the living room wearing Jenna's size-three coat, dancing and singing, "Fat guy in a little coat," which was from a popular movie at the time. I am so thankful we took the risk to have him. Our lives would not have been nearly as enriched without him.

CHAPTER 7

Last Chance

In this you greatly rejoice, though now for a little while
you may have had to suffer grief in all kinds of trials.
These have come so that your faith—of greater worth
than gold, which perishes even though refined by fire—
may be proved genuine and may result in praise, glory
and honor when Jesus Christ is revealed.

—1 Peter 1:6–7

I went back to school so many times I lost track. It took a span
of twelve years to get my undergraduate degree. The University of
Montana needed an assistant track coach during one of my returns to
school, so I applied. I was hired by the man who coached me during
the only cross country season I participated in at the U of M, right after
I was married. The pay from this position would be helpful with my
college expenses, not to mention it was very good for my resume. I was
to start coaching in January of 1988 when Chad was one year and three
months old. Knowing he was my last baby, I was having a hard time
giving up nursing him. In order to travel overnight with the team, I felt
it best if he were weaned, so it was probably a good thing.

After having been either pregnant or nursing continually for about
the past five and a half years, my breast size had increased over what
it had been when I was a runner. Though not overly huge, it was nice
to have *something*. As soon as I quit nursing Chad, the unthinkable
happened. My breasts were actually smaller, and now uglier, than before
I started having children. At first it was basically just loose skin that would
need time to shrink back to the original size, just as is necessary when
a person loses a substantial amount of weight. I was so embarrassed I
would turn around when dressing so Jim couldn't look at me without my
top on. This was disgusting. If only I could have somehow kept lactating

forever. I figured my breasts would return to their original size, but I had never anticipated this. Jim tried to encourage me by saying he found me attractive. He told me I shouldn't hide from him. After all, he was my husband. I was so self-conscious that I even tried to wear a shirt during intimacy. Jim wouldn't let me, so the next best thing was to position my arms so my breasts couldn't be seen or touched.

Being around all of the athletes on the track team, and not all that far removed from my own running career, made me long to finish something I had left undone. When I took Garrett to a track meet as a tiny baby, I left early because I couldn't stand to watch other people win *my* races. Now here I was, coaching young women in races I wished I was running in and felt I could win! At some point during the season, the head coach told me about a brand new track club that had started in Missoula that was designed to groom athletes for the Olympics. This couldn't be true in Montana! He also happened to be friends with the coach, so he connected us. I hadn't run much at all during the previous few years, due to being pregnant and uninspired, so I really didn't know what this man would say to me. We spoke during the winter, and the coach said, "Just start running every day, and if by June you still want to do it, you're in." Amazing! This sort of opportunity doesn't come around every day, or ever, for that matter. I felt so unworthy of such a blessing and was surprised there wasn't a requirement to at least run a few races first, to see if I still "had it." Miraculously, I was given another chance to realize my dreams.

The benefits of joining Mountain West Track Club were incredible. My schooling was paid for, and my training shoes (a dozen pairs per year) were paid for. My uniforms, travel bags, racing shoes, workout clothing, health club membership, massages, and even jogging bras were paid for. After I improved my times enough to be ranked nationally, I also started receiving a stipend to help with my living expenses. All of the travel costs to meets were also taken care of by the track club. Our coach owned his own planes, so on numerous occasions we were able to fly in catered comfort! I felt so humbled by all of these gifts. After being so destitute for the previous several years, I didn't even know how to accept it all.

The other women on the team seemed to be so at ease with the treatment, and eventually I was as well. The sad truth is that after a while, I actually started to expect it. If we normally received shoes or clothing at a certain time of year and we hadn't gotten them yet, I wondered when they would be coming. It's funny how quickly a person can become accustomed to a certain way of life. I try to remember this lesson often so I don't become ungrateful.

As time went on, I struggled with the strain I was under as a wife, mother of two very young boys, full-time student, and athlete. There were days when I devoted six hours to the sport in one way or another, along with all of my other daily duties. Although we didn't race year round, we did train twelve months out of the year. There were short morning runs of up to five miles and afternoon workouts, which I can hardly believe I was actually able to complete. I ran one hundred miles in a week for the first time in my life while competing for the club. We also lifted weights and were required to have a massage three times a week.

The massage was something we were chastised for if we didn't schedule. Needless to say, at no time was I in trouble for missing my massages. I'd never had one until I started running for Mountain West, and they were heavenly. The first time I arrived for my massage, I wasn't quite sure what to do. Feeling foolish, I asked the therapist what, if anything, I was supposed to wear during the massage. She was very kind, but I was pretty shy, especially due to how I viewed my body. It was hard to relax the first time or two. However, it didn't take long before I craved them. With what was expected of us physically, massage was incredibly important in order to stay healthy. It was a wonderful mental and emotional break from the daily stresses I faced as well.

We had our own athletic trainer who traveled with us to our meets. Since I had chronic problems with my calves and Achilles tendons, I received ultrasound or muscle stimulation treatments every day, along with taping. As wonderful as these benefits were, they all took precious time out of my already hectic life.

Our coach had gone through a divorce, so he enjoyed spending time with the team and would invite us out to dinner "just because." I was the only married person with children who was running for the track club at the time, so I felt no one really understood the pressure I was under to manage a household or life, for that matter. As nice as the offer to go out was, I had to get dinner ready for my family. I simply didn't have time to go out but felt guilty whenever I declined the invitation.

On one occasion, my workout took much longer than it was supposed to. It was January, when the days are short and darkness descends on us around 5:00 p.m. I went out for a long training run, leaving my kids in the daycare at the athletic club. I had pushed the pace on my twelve-mile run and was feeling good. The road I was running on had the river on one side and a snow-filled irrigation ditch adjacent to a mountain on the other. With a couple of miles to go, I noticed a truck parked, facing the same direction as I was headed, on the snow-packed road. The driver was out changing a flat tire. I waved and continued on.

About a mile farther up the road, a man drove up from behind with his window rolled down and said in a very sing-song and creepy way, "Jogging looks good." I am generally not too concerned about my safety, living in a place like Missoula, but something just didn't feel right about this. It is not uncommon to hear guys whistle at a female runner, but usually it's in the summer. It seemed very cold to be rolling a window down for that purpose. I tried to push any negative thoughts out of my mind until he stopped his car ahead of me and jumped out. I slowed my pace, unsure of what he was up to and not wanting to pass by him. My heart was racing abnormally fast as I watched him fling open the trunk and grab a tire-iron. Hoping he would leave before I overtook him, I began to memorize his license plate number. He jumped back in his car and sat there. I felt cornered because I was not about to jump into the icy cold river. Climbing a steep, snowy mountain was also not a great option. The man changing his flat tire was too far back, and there was no one else around. Hesitantly, I passed him as he sat there, not daring to look him in the eye. Then I picked up my pace until I was running as fast as I could go.

The next thing I knew, he flew by me at a high rate of speed in his car. I slowed as I watched his tail lights wind along the river road and up a small hill into the trees. I could see by the lights that the car had turned around, and instantly the headlights were shut off. The cat and mouse game had begun. I immediately turned and ran as fast as I was able, trying to get back to the man with the flat tire. Constantly looking over my shoulder in case he realized I was no longer coming, I continued to recite his license plate number. It was dark enough out that when a vehicle approached from the rear, I could not tell what type it was but could only see the headlights. Not wanting to take any chances, when a car approached, I would dive into the irrigation ditch, pressing my whole body into the snow until the vehicle would pass. I knew I needed to keep track of his whereabouts, so after each car went by, I peeked over the edge to see if it was him. When it wasn't, I would climb back out of the ditch and run for my life again.

My plan was to flag someone down if they were coming from in front of me. After going back and forth in my mind about whether I was crazy or this was a real threat, he finally came from behind me. Once he was safely past, I jumped out of the ditch and ran toward the athletic club, hoping to make it back to my children before he came looking for me again. No such luck. I was becoming weary physically, mentally, and emotionally. This man continued to drive back and forth, apparently searching for me. Each time he passed by, I would change directions, hoping someone would finally come from the right direction to save me. The last time, as I lay in the ditch, stiffening from the cold of the snow, I felt hopeless and helpless. The thought of my children waiting in the daycare and their mother never coming back kept running through my mind. My husband was at work by then, and no one would miss me until 7:00 p.m. when the daycare closed. By then it would be too late.

It finally occurred to me to pray. I had used all of my ingenuity to escape, but I was still trapped. After asking God to please send someone to get me, I took a deep breath and got back out of the ditch to run again. Finally, as I was again heading for the club, I saw headlights coming toward me instead of from behind. Probably looking like a person who was out of her mind, I practically ran in front of the vehicle, waving my arms wildly. I said to the driver, "Someone is after me. Could you give me a ride to the health club?" He told me to hop in, but since it was so icy and his tires were not that great, he would have to continue back to the stop sign a couple of miles away before he could turn around. I was so disturbed, I wasn't about to trust anyone, so I held onto the handle of the door, ready to jump out if he tried anything. As we drove along, he said, "I was fixing my flat tire and I noticed this guy driving back and forth. After I drove through, I wondered what happened to the woman who was running. I decided to come back and take a look." God had heard and answered my prayer!

When I finally made it home that night, I called my husband to tell him what happened. He said he felt like he should come and check on me before going to work but then shrugged it off, deciding he was sure I was fine. The Holy Spirit was working overtime on this one! I gave my husband the plate number and a description of the car. He worked for the sheriff's department at the time, so he ran the plate and found out who it was. We were so thankful I had trusted my instincts to hide, because this man was known by the law enforcement community quite well. My husband had previously booked him in jail for arson, assault, and aggravated assault when he was a jailer. It is hard to say what may have happened to me that night if God hadn't sent that wonderful man in the truck to save me. I was so shaken by the situation, I never even got his name, and I can't remember if I thanked him either.

This event changed how and where I chose to run for quite some time. I began by only running along this same road if Jim could ride beside me on his bike. Even running in different, more-populated locations made me a bit jumpy if I was training alone. After a while, I started feeling more comfortable working out with another female runner. Jim purchased pepper spray that easily clipped onto my shorts, so with that and my dog along, eventually I was able to run without another human. My heart would beat pretty fast in those instances until I finally reached an area with houses. The process of confronting my fears was long, and it took many months before I felt nearly back to normal. It really bothered me that someone like this could rob me of the freedom to go wherever I wanted without fear, but it didn't lessen my gratitude to God for saving me from that situation.

When you consider all of the time I spent each day on everything related to track, plus going to school, studying, cleaning, cooking, laundry, taking care of and playing with my kids, and traveling, my marriage was about to fall apart. Jim found it difficult when I was away so much and started putting pressure on me about my running. Being an athlete at that level is difficult, even with a lot of support. The stress between us brought out a lot of the old feelings of resentment I harbored against Jim from the past. I simply couldn't understand why he wouldn't back me in this. It was my last and best chance to realize my Olympic dream.

I think some of Jim's difficulty came from a sense of insecurity. I was getting in the best shape of my life and was finding fulfillment as my running times were steadily improving. He started to work out because he knew I would be around all those "hard bodies," as he would call them, at track meets. He became extremely fit and could run as many as nine miles at a pretty decent pace. I was traveling every other weekend all over the United States and sometimes into Canada, and he had always wanted to travel. Jim was picking up the slack at home too. I don't really know everything he was struggling with, but I do know one thing. He is extremely sorry he put pressure on me back then, but I can't entirely blame him. This was a lot for a young couple to deal with.

Yes, Jim even started changing diapers
when I was running for the track club. Here is the proof!

To this day, Jim says he wishes he would have married me early on and moved to Bozeman so I could have finished school and my track eligibility at Montana State. That is one of his greatest regrets. I believe, as Romans 8:28 says, "And we know that in all things God works for the good of those who love Him, who have been called according to His purpose." We may have made some poor decisions, but we became stronger people, and God never abandoned us. We also had wonderful children who blessed our lives and may never have been born if we'd chosen a different path.

Photo that appeared with a newspaper article about my return to running after I qualified for the National Track and Field Championships in June of 1989.

Another photo from the Missoulian, calling my husband and sons my
"support crew" as I was heading off to nationals.

The struggle over my running finally wasn't worth it anymore, so after two and a half years of competing and a poor finish at the national cross country championships, I left the club. The pressure from Jim was not the only thing contributing to my decision—it was just the easiest thing to blame since I still had old wounds concerning past sacrifices I'd made. The coach had planned an extended trip to Europe for the next summer so we would get used to lining up in races against people who did not speak the same language. That way, if any of us made it to the Olympics the following year, we would feel more comfortable in a similar situation. As wonderful as that opportunity was, being a mom of two little boys who cried because they didn't understand why Mommy was always leaving was heartbreaking to me. I nearly couldn't handle it when I went on the team's annual sixteen-day spring break trip to Florida. How would I cope with such an extended stay in Europe?

Now that I understand some of the problems a person with bipolar disorder faces, it is easier to realize why I made some of the choices I did, why I blamed people the way I did, and why I reacted to difficult situations the way I did.

One year when I was on the Florida trip, I had a meltdown. To begin with, I was missing my family terribly, in particular my kids. There is also a two-hour difference in time between Florida and Montana. Traveling through time zones can severely disrupt a person's brain chemistry since it throws off the sleep schedule. Last, the person I shared a condo with misinterpreted what was meant by some of my actions. That was the trigger that finally tipped me over the edge.

Our coach had supplied us with a powdered sports beverage, which we were required to drink periodically throughout each day to stay hydrated and keep our electrolytes at the proper levels. I had forgotten to pack mine, and fearing my coach's displeasure, I asked my condo-mate if I could use some of hers. The plan was to replace what I consumed upon returning home. She agreed, and I used it sparingly so as not to cause her to run out. Several days into our sixteen-day trip, I noticed a change in her attitude toward me. It seemed as though I needed to walk on eggshells around her, and it was starting to take its toll on me. Finally, one day she blew up at me with an accusation that I thought she was fat and I needed the sports drink for extra calories more than she did.

I crumbled emotionally. That thought had not even crossed my mind: I was just worried about being in trouble with the coach. One of my other teammates intervened and said it was a shame this happened to me, of all people. I'm fairly sure the intimation was that I was least able to handle my teammate's insecurities due to my own. Looking back on it now, this was very true. I had overreacted to her emotionally charged complaint by taking it too much to heart, which is typical for someone with bipolar disorder.

I have figured out what several of my triggers are, and unfairness is high on the list. It is not so much when it is an act of God, because I trust Him to know what is best for me. I found it difficult to deal with people who I believed were mean, lied to me or about me, or acted unjustly. I guess that's why I've always jumped in to protect weaker people. Unfortunately, I've learned life is often unfair, so my years as an adult have been extremely painful as I struggled with this disorder, all the while not knowing why.

The fact that a person suffering from bipolar disorder is very impulsive in their decision-making and has a hard time finishing things is what really robbed me of my Olympic dreams. I needed to take possession of my own decisions. Several of the other pressures I faced during this time were merely a byproduct of the disorder. The end of my running career was a painful loss that took many, many years to recover from. It required forgiveness and understanding toward my husband but ultimately toward myself.

CHAPTER 8

DEMONS IN THE TOY BOX

Rejoice in the Lord always. I will say it again: Rejoice!
Let your gentleness be evident to all. The Lord is near.
Do not be anxious about anything, but in everything,
by prayer and petition, with thanksgiving, present
your requests to God. And the peace of God, which
transcends all understanding, will guard your hearts
and your minds in Christ Jesus.

—Philippians 4:4–7

After leaving the track club, I finally did my student teaching. Hardly believing I was finished, I had my advisor double-check whether I had acquired all the credits necessary for graduation. I was in and out of college for such a long period of time that it seemed impossible it would ever end. But it was true, and I graduated with high honors! I was so excited to share this achievement with family members because it felt like such an accomplishment for me. Normally I don't get too excited about ceremonies, but this one felt pretty special because it took such determination to get there. All the way through high school, I hardly struggled with anything, but since that time it seemed like everything was difficult for me. I reflected back on what I'd been through emotionally, spiritually, physically, and financially over the past twelve years.

For a variety of reasons, no one in my very large extended family came to my graduation except for my husband and two young sons. Some people had very legitimate reasons for not attending. Others just didn't want to come, which of course can also be legitimate since I generally think graduations are boring anyway. I was pretty disappointed in this case, however, because the road getting there had been so bumpy for me. On the day of the ceremony, there were no gifts, there was no celebration, nothing. It gave me the feeling of a hollow victory since all of that time and effort had seemingly gone unnoticed.

For many years, I hadn't felt completely like a part of Jim's family. There were times when his sisters had invited me to lunch early on in our marriage, but I couldn't afford to go, so I declined. Maybe they figured I wouldn't go anyway, so the invitations ended for the most part unless it was something Jim was also invited to. I had my own sister living nearby, so I understand that it is natural to spend more time with your siblings than your in-laws. However, because of my insecurities, and possibly due to bipolar disorder, I was more sensitive about the issue than I should have been.

Graduation day was especially hard since one of Jim's sisters graduated prior to me, and six of his other siblings had come to town, even from other states, to attend the ceremony and have a barbecue. It had been a special time, and how I longed for that same attention. I'm sure if anyone had known what it meant to me, there would have been more family there. People aren't mind-readers, after all, and I could have expressed my wishes. Most who know me well understand I am not generally too excited about ceremonies, so why would this be any different? After all, consider my simple wedding. Since I unknowingly had bipolar disorder, it was always easiest to play the victim and blame others for my pain rather than to communicate effectively. I had to decide I wouldn't let it rob me of the feeling of accomplishment I was experiencing. Jim helped me by saying, "But we're here, and we are all that matter." He was right. After all was said and done, he and my boys were by my side, and they were proud of me. Most importantly, I was pleased with what I had finally accomplished.

Prior to student teaching, a friend had given me a book to read concerning which toys were not the best choices for your kids. Having a strong desire to be a good parent, and driven to perfection, I ended up having an extremely manic episode but didn't realize that's what it was until my diagnosis made sense of it many years later. I went through my kids' belongings, finding evil everywhere. Subsequently, much to their dismay, I began discarding their possessions. The boys collected GI Joes and a variety of other action figures. I thought the Cobras were evil, so I threw them away. After all, the serpent from the Garden of

Eden was wicked, and cobras are snakes, so it was necessary to get rid of them. I remember Garrett saying, "But they *are* evil. They're the bad guys. Who will the GI Joes fight if we don't have Cobras?" None of his pleading persuaded me. I threw away anything with a five-pointed star because I thought of a pentagram and even tossed their superman pajamas since my distorted thinking equated the superhero's flying with levitation. Books about Santa hit the trash can in the dark hours of the night, and their He-Man coloring books were tossed because the characters got their power from Gray Skull. Just from that name, it *had* to be evil, right? At the rate I was going, in a short period of time, they weren't going to have any toys left.

Not only were the kids distressed about sacrificing their belongings, but I also frightened them by my demeanor. One night we decided to have a slumber party in the living room, but really it was because of the fact that I was so paranoid I didn't want to lose sight of my kids during the hours of darkness. Thankfully, throwing the boys' toys away is the only time I recall scaring my kids due to having bipolar disorder.

Throughout this three-day episode, I couldn't sleep or slow my thinking, and I spoke really, really fast. I thought I had some kind of insight no one else had and it was my duty to help them understand. Now I realize this is part of the grandiose feeling someone with bipolar disorder experiences. At one point, Jim put me in a great big bear hug and told me I needed to slow down. I could feel my heart pounding rapidly, and I was squirming to get away. There was too much that needed to be done! On Sunday morning, I knew the pastor of our church went early to pray. Feeling I should share this new-found knowledge, preferably with the whole church, I drove there at 7:00 a.m. and interrupted his prayer time. Pastor told me I could speak at the service later in the morning but suggested I go home and get my thoughts more organized. I can only imagine what he was thinking! What surprises me is that he was actually going to let me speak to a church with several hundred people in attendance.

I couldn't wait to prepare something to share at church. Afterward, I asked Jim how he thought it went, and he said it was fine, except I might want to talk slower next time. I must not have sounded totally crazed, though, because a high school student from a local Christian school was

81

there and told his dad about it. This man was the superintendent, so he invited me to come to their next teacher in-service meeting. By the time I shared with them, the manic episode was over and I was feeling quite foolish for how pushy I'd been. I gave the teachers a toned-down version of it at their in-service and was relieved when it was finally over. I wanted to crawl in a hole and forget it had ever happened. For a while, it was difficult to face people who had been at church that Sunday. Not only was this episode embarrassing, but it also cost me financially. Feeling guilty for what I had put the boys through, I bought them some new toys. Jim recently revealed that he too made a habit of buying the kids a new action figure every time he took them to the store to make up for what I had done. I always just thought he was a soft touch, which I believe is still partly true!

There was an odd feeling in my brain as I came back to a balanced place that time. It seemed as if cobwebs were disappearing from inside my head. I could almost hear a crackling sound as my brain was becoming less clouded. I began to think more and more clearly and was so embarrassed. What had I just done? As foolish as I felt from this incident, I rationalized that it was simply part of maturing and growing as a person. I was determined to learn from my mistakes and not repeat them again. This episode caused me to question my lucidity somewhat if I thought about it too much, and it was quite a humbling experience. I hoped I could trust myself in the future. I would simply have to try harder and also rely on my husband more to know whether I was thinking correctly. Little did I know this illness would twist and show up in different ways. No matter how great the attempt, I could not outgrow it, and the energy I expended in my endeavor to keep the mania hidden was extremely tiring. Thankfully, my laid-back husband loved me throughout, and the incident was not shoved in my face, as I had a habit of doing to him when he made mistakes.

After student teaching in the spring, I applied for a position at the same Christian school where I had previously shared at the in-service. I landed a job teaching sixth grade half-time and coaching high school track. Garrett would transfer from public school to third grade there in the fall, and Chad would go to daycare. It was a tough transition for me and also for the kids in many ways. My marriage would be put to the test once again, and it wouldn't be the last time.

CHAPTER 9

INDECISION

If any of you lacks wisdom, he should ask God, who gives generously to all without finding fault, and it will be given to him. But when he asks, he must believe and not doubt, because he who doubts is like a wave of the sea, blown and tossed by the wind. That man should not think he will receive anything from the Lord: he is a double-minded man, unstable in all he does.

—James 1:5–8

My first year as a junior high school teacher was difficult. Weary of having Chad in daycare while finishing my undergraduate work and running for the track club, I just wanted to be a mom for a while. I still yearned to have more children, but we made the decision to permanently eliminate that possibility after Chad was born. Not to mention, teachers take piles of work home. Being a perfectionist, and certain it could always be done better, I had a tendency to push myself to exhaustion while never feeling a sense of completion.

Coaching was also a challenge. I was the head high school girls' coach, and another person was the head boys' coach. My background was in distance running, but I had the task of working with all of the boys and girls in the throwing events, hurdles, and sprints. The other coach's personal experience was in the hurdles, but he was working with the distance runners. We had an assistant who coached the long, triple, and high jumpers.

This division of duties didn't make much sense to me, but the other head coach was there first and wanted to work with the distance runners, so the superintendent said to go along with it. This was not what I expected when I was hired. I did as much research as I could so I would be able to help the athletes in my charge, but I felt totally inadequate, especially since I was coaching some very talented kids. It was frustrating to watch the other coach working with the distance runners, inasmuch as it would have been second nature to me. I felt more like his assistant than his equal most of the time, because he sort of knew the ropes at this school and was a take-charge type of person.

The boys' coach once asked me to pick up some new spikes for the athletes' shoes from a sporting goods store. He wrote down the size of the spikes and how many he wanted on a note. I noticed that the ones he was asking for were not allowed on the next track we would be competing on, so I assumed we needed them for the meet after that. Since it had been such a busy week for me, I thought I would wait to pick them up until I had a bit more time. On the bus heading to the meet, he asked if I had remembered to pick up the spikes. I said I hadn't done it but would make sure to do so before we needed them at the next meet. He *blew up*! Right in front of the kids, he got after me for not following his directions. Trying to explain my thought process, he cut me off mid-sentence. I felt so embarrassed in front of the athletes, since they didn't know the whole story. I was not inept, which is how I continually felt around him, and this was really not my fault since he'd written the wrong size spikes on the note. I wanted to defend myself, but it was pointless. Coaching with this man was truly a challenge—one I did not enjoy at all.

I must admit that coaching the events I was not terribly familiar with wasn't all bad, since it stretched me and I did learn a lot. Our boys team took second overall at the state meet, with only two athletes competing in multiple events. One was a hurdler and one was a distance runner, so with two individual state champs and a team trophy, I guess we didn't ruin them entirely.

Though technically I was only working part-time, it certainly didn't seem like it. We had a teachers' meeting before school every day of the week and an in-service every Wednesday after school. I taught in the morning, so I would return for the afternoon meeting and for practice during the coaching season. Being a small, private school meant there was no public funding, so we all pitched in to make it work. Coaches were unpaid, there were no recess duty aides, so we took turns, and the kids ate lunch in the classroom with their teacher, which in this case was me since I was the morning teacher. We were required to get our chauffeur's license so we could drive the buses if necessary. Coaches always drove the kids to a nearby track for practice, since our school didn't have one, and also drove to all of the track meets. As a first-year teacher, I had to work very hard on lesson plans, plus I took papers home to grade. It seemed a lot like full-time employment to me.

My feelings about having more children intensified, so without my husband's approval, I looked both into having my tubal ligation reversed and in-vitro fertilization. I was told that my former doctor had removed my fallopian tubes altogether, so there was no way to re-attach them. I was not completely sure how I felt about in-vitro, but it was definitely cost prohibitive anyway.

We heard about some different situations where children might need to be adopted, but I was extremely disappointed when nothing came to fruition. I cried at a school in-service meeting because another teacher shared something from Scripture that made me feel God was telling me no about adoption. To me it meant a set of twin girls due to come home from the hospital soon were not going to be mine. I can't remember what the verse was, but the message was very clear: what would I be willing to give up in order to be in God's will? Jim hadn't been completely sold on the idea of twins anyway, but I was pushing ahead with it. That should have been a clue it wasn't right, but I so desperately wanted those children. It was a good thing God was preparing my heart that these girls would not be my daughters due to the impending tragedy.

I was worried for the welfare of the twins' older brother, since he was not going to be removed from the home at that time. I prayed somehow he would escape too, because it sounded like a dreadful situation. I was extremely disappointed when the parents were allowed to take the babies home even though their own friends and family were concerned. Not long after, both of the infant girls died the same night. They were in the care of their very young father at the time. It seemed suspicious that two healthy babies would die of SIDS simultaneously. The father had a criminal record and was violent at times, but the cause of death was inconclusive. I had so wanted to rescue those babies, but there was one positive outcome: the little boy was placed in a very loving home. Sadly, the baby girls appeared to have sacrificed their lives for their brother.

We learned of another adoption opportunity after I decided not to return as a teacher the next year. Jim and I had already applied to become foster parents when we heard about a beautiful little two-and-a-half-year-old girl needing a family. Some friends of ours connected us with her grandma, who was taking care of her at that time. This woman loved her granddaughter dearly but decided she wanted her to have a complete family. She had several very specific requirements for the new family, and we fit every single one of them. We scheduled a meeting with the grandma and the little girl at a park in a nearby town. She was adorable. With blue eyes and blond hair like my boys, she was projected to be six feet tall at maturity, exactly my height. It seemed like a perfect match in every possible way. The grandma felt at ease with us and we with her. She still very much wanted to be the little girl's grandma after the adoption as well. The interesting thing was that I had a check in my spirit, like something wasn't right about proceeding, but I did not voice my feelings to Jim. I couldn't really put my finger on it because everything seemed perfect, so I kept it to myself since I desperately wanted more children.

Because we'd already begun the foster care application process and the same organization in the other town was involved in this little girl's case, I felt it was appropriate to contact our social worker in Missoula concerning our desire to adopt her. After the initial excitement over our foster parent application, the caseworker said, "Why would we place her with you when you would take any child? She is a desirable child. Anyone would want her." Apparently, being willing to accept foster children of any age from any background actually hurt our chances to adopt this little girl. The agency was so short on available foster homes that she made it clear she didn't want to lose us as a resource if we chose to adopt instead. But what about what was best for *this* child? The next time I spoke with the caseworker from the other location, he seemed hesitant. This was different from how he had previously acted. After speaking with the Missoula office, he said it would not be possible for us to be considered as a placement for this little girl.

This was a grave injustice to me. We thought about withdrawing as potential foster parents altogether. That would show them you can't treat people unfairly! In the end, Jim and I decided to proceed with our plan to do foster care, since all that would be accomplished by leaving the program was to make one less home available for children who desperately needed one. I actually handled this better than some other possibly lesser injustices, but it still wasn't easy since unfairness is one of my triggers. Maybe the fact that we would be having other children come to live with us softened the blow of losing this opportunity for adoption, along with the unexplainable uncertainty I felt after meeting with the little girl and her grandma.

We ended up having two little boys for several months that year. They were half-brothers and also had two more siblings in other foster homes. Four little boys from the age of three and a half on down, each with different fathers, shared a twenty-one-year-old mother. Eventually all of these boys would need to be placed permanently in a family. We had the oldest of the brothers with us, and it was hardest on Chad since they took his place as the baby of the family. There was definitely some jealousy, but when the prospect of adoption materialized, I thought we could make it work in spite of Jim's misgivings. I think what finally made the decision for us concerning whether we should adopt them was when I started pushing Jim toward adopting all four of the brothers! He was not quite up to the idea of having six boys, especially so many little ones. It was so typical of me to turn a positive thing into something much too big to handle. Since Jim and I had differing opinions on which course to take, we chose not to pursue adoption at that time. In the end, our foster sons were placed with a childless couple.

After only one year of the ups and downs of foster care, and six children later, I decided to go back to teaching. This was mostly due to the struggles we faced having our own young children exposed to some difficult situations with a couple of the older kids. We could house up to three foster children at one time, and it was hard to say no when a child needed a place to stay. We didn't always use good judgment when accepting placements, thus overextending ourselves. Each story tugs at your heart, but the timing was a little off for us. I was re-hired at the same school, except it was full-time teaching instead of part-time, plus coaching.

It was very typical of me to change the direction of my life from the age of nineteen on. I seemed to be unable to stick with anything for very long due to stress, boredom, or discontent. Praying to God for wisdom, I continually felt tossed about like a wave of the sea, as the verse from James 1 describes. I so desired to know what contentment and stability felt like. Would it ever be possible for me to be anything but double-minded and unstable?

CHAPTER 10

LIFE AS MRS. JOHNSON

Endure hardship as discipline; God is treating you as sons. For what son is not disciplined by his father? If you are not disciplined (and everyone undergoes discipline), then you are illegitimate children and not true sons. Moreover, we have all had human fathers who disciplined us and we respected them for it. How much more should we submit to the Father of our spirits and live! Our fathers disciplined us for a little while as they thought best; but God disciplines us for our good, that we may share in his holiness. No discipline seems pleasant at the time, but painful. Later on, however, it produces a harvest of righteousness and peace for those who have been trained by it.

—Hebrews 12:7–11

The next six years were quite possibly the hardest years of my life. An estimated 75 to 90 percent of people suffering from bipolar disorder have difficulty working, and I was no exception. I had a history of starting, stopping, and re-starting jobs on a regular basis but always with some way of justifying my decisions. Some of the teaching staff did not stay very long at this school, possibly because the pay was not great but the responsibilities were. For those who did not need to increase their salaries and had stability in their teaching schedules each year, it seemed to go fairly well. I was not so fortunate. Every year my schedule changed, so I found myself prepping as though I was a first-year teacher. Expecting excellence in my teaching made this a daunting task. Add in an undiagnosed mental illness and a husband who repeatedly subcontracted houses for us to live in, and it was a recipe for disaster.

We moved to a new house during each of the first four seasons I was a coach at this school. Stability is incredibly important to someone who suffers from bipolar disorder. I found it difficult to stay organized while struggling to pack and unpack boxes, and my memory was failing me at times. During one of these moves, I inadvertently hurt my sister's feelings.

Garrett was in baseball, plus track season had already begun for me. Most of our belongings had been packed for the next move. Out of the blue, Jim's mom called to ask if they could take Garrett along on a trip out of state for our niece's wedding. They were leaving the next day. I didn't want him to go so far without us, especially on such short notice, so I was trying to think of every reason he shouldn't. What about baseball practice? What about homework? What about his clothes? As Jim and I discussed it, I wearily started doing laundry, just in case. Jim had an answer for everything. I felt like I was forgetting something important, but Jim said, "You're making excuses. Just let him go." Finally, with a nagging feeling I hadn't recalled something, there was no other argument, and the next morning he was gone.

After school on the day he left, I spoke with my sister on the phone. She mentioned something about her son's birthday party, and I gasped. That was the thing I had forgotten. If I could have brought Garrett back right then, I would have, but it was too late. When she invited him to the party, she had gone out of her way to make sure it was on a day he could come. They had recently moved to Missoula, so Garrett's cousin hadn't made a lot of friends yet. They were buddies, and it was really important for him to attend. I was sick while telling her where he was. Needless to say, she was disappointed, and I felt like the biggest heel ever. For people who suffer from bipolar disorder, absentmindedness is not uncommon, especially in stressful situations. It is then followed by feelings of inadequacy or guilt because of the consequences. Though I was only in my early thirties at the time, I learned to write important things down after that. Then the challenge became remembering where I put the notes.

Since I personally felt like a failure, I assumed that's also how others viewed me. One instance of this surfaced when I received a letter from my mom concerning the fact that Garrett had missed his cousin's birthday party. Jim handed it to me unopened. As I read about her disappointment that I would allow my son to go on the trip and in effect, take a better offer, I let out a guttural cry. After being my parents' shining star, for a long time I had suspected that I'd failed them. Here was the proof in black and white. Jim asked me, "What happened?" When I told him, he said with relief, "Oh, I thought someone died." My tear-filled response was, "Someone did, and it was me." A healthy person would have simply called and explained what happened, but I was filled with excruciating pain and tucked it away with all of the other emotional injuries that were burying me.

Along with the hardships, teaching at this school was also wonderful in many ways. I made lifelong friends and was able to teach and coach the most amazing students a teacher could ever hope for. I started a cross country program for the high school boys and girls while there. In the second year of its existence, my boys' team won the state title and the girls took second place in their race. Several athletes made the all-state team. It was a wonderful experience I will never forget, especially the completion of the boys' race.

In order to get in a good position to see the finish line on this particular course, it was necessary to miss almost the entire last mile of the race. My boys were all in pretty good position going into the final mile, but a lot can happen during that critical stage of the race. I opted to get a great view of the finish. Nervously waiting for the kids to come over the final hill and down to the finish line, I finally saw the leader. It was a really gifted runner from another school, which was no surprise to anyone. After a short time, the second place runner came over the hill, and he was one of mine! He had advanced several places in the last mile. Right after that, another athlete came over the rise, and he also was wearing our school jersey. Then the fourth place runner appeared. Yes, he too was a boy on my team. Every single runner on our team had advanced in their position during that last mile. After all was said and done, four out of our five scoring runners made the all-state team by placing in the top fifteen while helping us to win the state championship. This was more satisfying than any individual state title I'd ever won, since we could all celebrate this victory together. No other high school team from Missoula had ever won a state cross country team title before.

The boys were the 1995 state champions in cross country.

My girls took second place at the state cross country meet in 1995.

Another memorable occurrence during my first year of teaching at this school was when both of the sixth grade classes combined at Christmastime to bless a less-fortunate family from our community. We found this mom and her four children in a newspaper column called, "Who Cares?" She lived in a single-wide trailer, and none of her appliances worked, not even the stove or refrigerator. Her husband was an alcoholic and not present in the home. Their disabled daughter used a wheelchair and was becoming too heavy for the mom to carry inside, but they had no wheelchair ramp. The youngest child, an infant, was the result of a rape, yet she chose to have and raise her in spite of her dire financial condition. They had no Christmas tree or decorations, and the children were not getting any presents this year. Our students and their families went all out for this dear woman. We were able to secure all new appliances or fix the existing ones. Some dads built a wheelchair ramp, and we gave her a tree with all of the lights and decorations she would need. There were boxes and boxes of clothing and toys, both new and gently used, plus food for Christmas dinner and beyond. Each student carried in at least two to three boxes, filled to the brim, before we were finished.

We also decided to sing Christmas carols, and some of the students shared Scripture. I asked my class if any of them had a special verse they would like to read. Two very sweet girls decided they wanted to read Matthew 6:25–34, which talks about worrying. Well, I was worried about having them share this! It speaks of how the birds don't worry about what they are to eat or wear and that a person is more important than they are, so why worry? Because of the way it was written, I thought it may come across harshly, since we had so much more than she. This poor woman had been through a great deal, and I didn't want to make her feel as though we were scolding her if she had some concerns. After all, I didn't know if she even believed in God, and I would be more than a bit stressed if I were in her circumstance. I asked the girls if they were sure this was what they wanted to share, that maybe something about God's love would be nice or about Christ being born. They firmly said, "No, this is the one we want to share." These two girls were normally so passive and sweet that I was a bit surprised about their conviction. With some reservation, I allowed them to use that passage of Scripture.

The delivery day was a wonderful experience. A few parents came along, and it felt so good to bless this deserving family. After taking box after box of items inside, we sang the songs and shared the Scripture verses. When the girls read the passage from Matthew, the mom went into the home crying. Uh oh, I knew we'd blown it. Why hadn't I made those girls switch to something else? It turned out that she was crying because she had recently read that very Scripture, and she knew God was telling her He would be with her and take care of her needs. What a relief! The girls had been right all along. This turned out to be one of the most unforgettable experiences of my life, and I think my students would agree. One boy was so excited that he asked if we could do it again.

I learned so much about God's Word while at this school because we were immersed in it daily. We also had the privilege of being able to teach about God in each class, which is a precious freedom to be given.

There were, however, several great difficulties for me during this time. I routinely spent up to seventy hours working each week, especially during coaching seasons, and we moved from home to home continuously. By the time track season came around, I was so exhausted I hardly had the energy to go to church. It was my only day to catch up on laundry and housework and maybe cook a decent meal. Also, now as a police officer, my husband was on shift work, so we rarely saw each other. I had young sons to care for, and I expected too much of myself. Add in bipolar disorder, and I was an absolute mess most of the time, whether other people could see it or not. I said, "I hate my life" to my husband more times than I can count during those years. Jim would routinely say, "Just be happy for me." Trying to lighten the mood, at times he would mimic me, and in a high-pitched, shaky voice say, "I hate my life," causing the boys to laugh. Unfortunately, all it did was make me feel even more isolated and wounded. Jim did not realize how desperate I was becoming.

During moments alone, I would grab my head out of frustration, holding onto my hair as though it were a handle. It was all I could do to refrain from hitting my head with an open hand. I didn't dare let anyone know about this because I knew it was strange behavior, to say the least, but I felt I would nearly burst during the most stressful times. I constantly wanted to resign from my position. Jim preferred I teach, however, and I thought his reasons were selfish. He would tell me, "One more year. I want a boat." I was crumbling more and more each day until I finally walked into the superintendent's office, ready to quit. I guess my boss could see what a disaster I was and told me to take the next four Fridays off. That helped me make it through the coaching season, but it was still a tremendous struggle.

Over a several-year period, during the summer months, two of our nephews came from another state to visit Jim's mom. The boys happened to be about the same ages as our boys, so as soon as they arrived at their grandparents', they would immediately begin begging to come to our house. We had things for them to do, and it was fun for the cousins to get to play with each other. It was enjoyable taking them camping, swimming, hiking, and floating the river with us. As much as I wanted to have the kids visit, it became difficult to keep them for the larger part of the summer, since I was so overwhelmed during the school year and was trying to recover from the stress.

I asked Jim if we could call his sister, since the boys always ended up spending the time with us rather than at their grandparents. That way we could set up when and for how long the kids would visit. It's not that I didn't want them to come. I simply wanted to work out the details with his sister since it affected us, and truthfully me, the most. He refused and told me she would just get mad. I didn't think that would be the case, so I offered to call her myself. He forbade me from contacting her. His reaction was very frustrating for me and added to my feelings of not having any say in what was happening in my life. It seemed as though he was more worried about how his sister might feel about it than I did. However, a special bond between the boys was the wonderful result of the kids getting to spend so much time together. Especially in that respect, I am very thankful to have given them the opportunity to know each other well.

After I was well-received by one of the administrators for several years, something seemed to change in our working relationship. There was one instance when an angry parent called me with a complaint concerning his daughter, who was in my class. He then continued on his rampage by calling this administrator. My boss completely had my back and defended me. The next day, the father called me again to apologize since he found out his daughter had fabricated the story. Then, for some unknown reason to me, everything changed.

When my dog had a litter of puppies, a student of mine was interested in purchasing one. On a Saturday morning, while the puppies were still so small their eyes were shut, there was a basketball game at the school. This student's mom would be in attendance, and we currently lived on the next block, so I decided to wrap one of them up and walk over to the gym. When this same administrator saw all of the women oohing and aahing and passing the puppy around in a towel, he came over and asked who it belonged to. I told him it was one from our litter. He continued by scolding me in front of everyone for bringing an animal into the school and instructed me to take it right back home. I did as I was told, but I was so confused, embarrassed, and even hurt by this. I noticed the moms seemed taken aback by what he said too. In retrospect, I was not the one who should have felt humiliated by what was said. After all, this was a contradiction, since kids brought pets to show and tell, several teachers had classroom pets, and even he often brought his own large dog to the school on weekends.

There were several other occasions when I felt publicly embarrassed by this person. I was harshly reprimanded in the main office in front of the secretaries, students, and a copy machine repairman. I was also scolded as I sat in the bleachers at one of my son's basketball games by one of the other administrators. Garrett and a boy from the other team each had a hold of the ball, and as my son tried to pull it away from him, the other boy did not let go. Garrett was so much larger than most other kids his age that he sent this boy flying horizontally for quite a number of feet. When this happened a second time with the same kid, an assistant principal was seated behind me to the right, and he jokingly asked what I'd been feeding Garrett. I smiled and maybe even let out a little laugh as I shrugged my shoulders.

Another administrator made his way into the stands, and facing me, he loudly stated that I should be ashamed of myself for how I was acting at this game, apparently due to my startled reaction to Garrett's strong play. I had invited my sister and her son to the game with me, and I have to say, they were unimpressed by that. I couldn't figure out what I had done to warrant the treatment I was receiving from a couple of my superiors. Even if I was doing something wrong, to publicly embarrass an employee did not seem right. I worked hard to make sure I did not do the same thing to my students, but if I realized I may have embarrassed them, I apologized immediately. These experiences actually caused me to become a better teacher.

I received counseling at various points during my teaching career. When these things were happening to me at work, I spoke to my pastor about it. I told him I believed a couple of the administrators thought I was weak. He said, "No, it is the opposite. I believe they think you are strong and feel that your will needs to be broken." Sad to say, I don't know how much more broken I could have been.

Marriages need more time and attention to thrive than we were able to give ours under these circumstances. Although I was constantly surrounded by people, I was incredibly lonely. There was one school year when the only time Jim and I had a day off together during the entire nine months was during Christmas break. That does not bode well for closeness between a husband and wife. I felt like a single parent most of the time since my schedule was closer to the kids' schedules. Jim was on a rotation, often working nights and weekends. He also coached boys' basketball in the winter, which chipped away at any spare time we may have had for each other.

During my teaching years, I acquired quite a number of pets. We had dogs, cats, rabbits, hamsters, fish, guinea pigs, and rats, several of them at the same time. The greatest number of dogs we owned at one time was four, not counting when we had a litter of puppies. Of course, being the walking Humane Society that I am, this is not too hard to imagine. The problem was, since they were pretty much my idea, the responsibility of caring for them landed on my shoulders. I believe the impetus for collecting all of these animals was two-fold. First, I could no longer bear children when I originally would have enjoyed having a large family, and second, I was emotionally deprived due to the gulf between my husband and myself. Animals will invariably love you no matter what you do. They are always happy to see you and crave your affection. Somehow, by acquiring them I was attempting to fill a void in my life, but it wasn't necessarily wise. I probably would have had even more pets if Jim hadn't put the brakes on at times since I am such a pushover for a puppy.

Bipolar disorder is marked by a strong desire to escape when life seems too unbearable. I believed I could never escape the agony I was experiencing as a teacher. I was trying to please God in every way, so I felt it necessary to submit to my husband's wishes concerning my teaching career. Jim didn't want me to quit, so I was stuck. Though the thought occasionally popped into my mind, I had not seriously considered taking my own life since I was nineteen, and I cared way too deeply for my sons to leave them anyway. The only manner of escape I could think of would be if God decided to take Jim's life. Then I wouldn't have to do what Jim wanted.

I am not at all proud of having this thought but will be as transparent as possible in an attempt to shed some light on the twisted thinking of people who suffer with mental illness. I had moments of such desperation that I actually prayed God would deliver me from what felt like a life sentence by ending my husband's life. It hadn't occurred to me I could pray for God to open Jim's mind to see the anguish I was experiencing. God's Word talks about wives submitting to their husbands, but the husband is supposed to love his wife like Christ loved the church. The second part of the verse is sometimes ignored. That is a sacrificial love, but I was the one feeling sacrificed.

After praying such a terrible prayer, I was shaken to the core. I rarely watched TV during those years because I didn't have time for such a luxury, but for some reason I turned on the news one night while Jim was at work. They were covering a local story as it was unfolding involving a shooter who had gunned down a Missoula police officer. I couldn't believe what I was seeing. They wouldn't say whether the officer was dead or alive, but they showed the face of the shooter as soon as he was captured. Garrett said, "If that guy shot my dad, I'm going to kill him." If Jim happened to be the officer who was shot and were to die, I would feel totally to blame. How could I ever live with that guilt? I couldn't really hope it was someone else either. These fellow officers were his friends.

I kept pacing back and forth from the TV to look out the front window. I figured they wouldn't call me with this news but would instead pull up in the driveway. Jim hadn't been wearing his bulletproof vest during that time because it didn't fit well and was uncomfortable.

I went to look for it, and there it was, in the closet. This was not good. I couldn't stand it anymore. Though I knew I shouldn't during a crisis, I called the city desk. The lady I spoke with told me she didn't know who the officer was and had no details. I hung up the phone and thought, *Yeah, right. She just didn't want to tell me the truth over the phone.* About forty-five minutes later, Jim called to tell me he was okay. What a relief, but who was it then? It turned out to be a sergeant who had responded to a call that was intended for Jim.

All of the street officers had been busy on other calls, so Jim had to leave his zone to deal with a little fender bender. He was about to clear and return to his own area when the call about the gunman came in. The sergeant got on the radio and offered to respond, and then Jim said he would back him. The next thing Jim heard on the radio as he hurried there were the words, "Officer down, officer down!" A kid who had witnessed the shooting ran over and used the wounded officer's radio. Jim raced to the location as quickly as he could. It was a tragic sight. His sergeant, his friend, was face-down on the pavement. The officer ended up becoming completely paralyzed from the incident, as the bullet had hit his neck. Unfortunately, his vest hadn't protected him this time. Needless to say, I never prayed that Jim would die ever again. I was a bit shaken, and God made it clear to me that it was not his time to go yet.

Jim in his dress uniform the night he received the Life Saving Medal for his actions when his fellow officer was shot in the line of duty.

According to my doctor, the stress I was under during my years of teaching caused some physical problems for me. A heavy menstrual cycle plagued me each school year but would lighten during the summer. Anemia was one difficulty I faced, which left me prone to illness and without the energy necessary to complete my tasks. I tried going on the pill, but it didn't completely take care of the problem, and it wasn't necessary for birth control anyway. Another year I had a surgical procedure called a D & C, which was supposed to lessen the bleeding. It helped for a while, but the difficulties returned.

My last resort was to have a hysterectomy. I hadn't been ready to make such a huge decision for several years because I knew it would definitely end my ability to bear children. Though still quite young to have to undergo this drastic of a measure, I was very weary of struggling, so I finally believed it was necessary. I made the decision in January after enduring a heavy period lasting forty days. Because it was deemed elective surgery by the school, I was not allowed to have time off. With a less-than-positive attitude, I waited until the school year ended in June. If the man making the decision had experienced what I was living through, I didn't think he would feel it was at all elective. The surgery was a good decision but certainly wasn't the cure for all that ailed me.

In May of the previous school year, Chad had actually influenced me as I came to grips with the fact I would not have any more children. That's what finally made it possible for me to go through with the hysterectomy. Chad was in third grade at the time, and they were making heart pins for Mother's Day. The hearts were constructed out of layer upon layer of colored paper glued together and then clear-coated with some sort of epoxy that would harden and protect them. The children then sanded the hearts prior to putting the final clear coat on them to bring out each color of paper they'd chosen. This created a unique pattern, and they were quite attractive.

When I saw all of the other moms' hearts, I thought they were really pretty colors and sanded so nicely. Chad had chosen red, black, and white. Those seemed like interesting colors for Mother's Day, plus he had sanded the middle of the heart so hard it looked like a bullet had pierced the center. I didn't think too much about it, but later on as I studied it, something profound occurred to me. That's what my heart looked like. I still had a gaping wound in my heart, not only from the loss of my son Brent but also from the loss of any future children I could have. Then I considered the colors Chad had chosen. Black, which was the dominant color, signified loss to me. The red seemed to represent sacrifice because of the blood of Jesus on the cross. The center of the bullet hole was filled with white. I started to cry as I thought maybe God was telling me to fill the hole in my heart with Him. That was certainly a day of healing for my broken heart. I was finally able to begin finding contentment in the two wonderful sons God was allowing me to raise.

Jim and I often spent our precious few moments together arguing during my teaching years. I was frustrated since I'd always been able to accomplish what I set out to do. It seemed other teachers fared better than me, however. The students and parents were fond of me, and I'm sure most had no idea how tortured I was. During one of our disagreements, Jim suggested we drive to the superintendent's house to see if he could help us settle the dispute concerning whether I should be teaching any longer.

As we drove along, there was a woman biking on the shoulder of the road. Feeling as though I might explode, I had an extremely strong urge to swerve and hit her. I'm not sure if it was because of all the suppressed anger I was experiencing that made me want to hurt anyone in my path. Maybe it was due to feeling I had no control over anything in my life and it would give me momentary power. I'm not entirely sure. At any rate, it is a good thing Jim was driving because it was all I could do to refrain from grabbing the wheel from him. Once we were past her, as quickly as the impulse arrived, it went away. How could I have entertained such an idea, even for such a brief moment? I was intensely shaken by the thought.

In 1999, when it was time to sign our covenants to teach for the next year, I begged Jim to let me quit teaching. I promised him that if he truly prayed and laid this decision before the Lord, I would submit to whatever he decided was best. He agreed to do so. I honestly thought this was a safe bet. There was no way God would want me to continue slaving away at the school while my own children were being neglected. They were my first calling as a mom. After a week or two passed and the decision had to be made, Jim told me he felt God wanted me to continue to teach. I *could not* believe it! How could this be? God had let me down. This was the one time in my life I was mad at God. I had trusted Him to speak to my husband's heart, but He didn't do it.

Desperate to survive, I gave up coaching during my last year of teaching. This was a painful decision for me, and it was even more difficult to convince the superintendent this was necessary. Because of my love for the sport and the athletes, it was easy for me to invest my life into coaching, but unfortunately, we were not paid for it. Needing to remove something from my schedule, but still requiring some income, the obvious choice was to relinquish my coaching duties. If I were to be able to manage in this occupation, I needed to focus my energies on teaching alone. I truly thought I might be able to salvage my career, so with a renewed zeal, I approached the beginning of the school year.

As the new year was set to begin, I was informed I would be teaching junior high PE over the Internet to students all around the world, in addition to my other courses. First of all, I had never even emailed anyone before. Let alone, how in the world do you teach an active class like PE over the Internet? I found out about my new duties on a Friday and was supposed to be up and running on Monday. My zeal immediately turned to anger. It didn't seem to matter what I did, I would always feel overloaded as a teacher. My attitude was terrible. Interestingly, I never felt attacked or humiliated by any of my superiors the entire school year. If that had been the case, I would have let loose. In fact, I was waiting for the opportunity. Because of my anger and disappointment about even being there, I was no longer concerned with pleasing God or man. If it weren't for the teacher in charge of the Internet school being so kind and patient, I doubt I would have ever shown up at the computer lab to teach my class. Thank you, Barry, for putting up with me in that most difficult of all years. When the school year was over, I knew I was done. I was a terribly crippled individual and have never taught or coached since.

CHAPTER 11

DESERTED

Therefore, as God's chosen people, holy and dearly loved, clothe yourselves with compassion, kindness, humility, gentleness and patience. Bear with each other and forgive whatever grievances you may have against one another. Forgive as the Lord forgave you. And over all these virtues put on love, which binds them all together in perfect unity.

—Colossians 3:12–14

Jim came from a very large, close-knit family of nine kids. When we were dating and I decided to return to Bozeman for school during winter quarter, his sisters did something I will never forget. It was Christmas, and they showered me with gifts. What made it all the more meaningful was the fact I was so lonely and despondent about my relationship with Jim. I didn't know all of his seven sisters well yet, which made it so much more unexpected and special. It caused me to nearly cry because I was so overcome with the kindness that was shown. I hadn't felt that loved in what seemed like such a long time. Later on, when Brent died, they purchased a very dressy suit, shoes included, for me to wear to the memorial service. I had nothing appropriate to wear in my closet because of our financial condition, so this too was a wonderful and meaningful gift.

Everyone adored Jim's parents. His mom had an impish grin and a cute little personality. Vivian was sort of like a dorm mother to the college kids while she worked there as a custodian, and she wasn't afraid to give them advice on any topic. She would do anything for her children and absolutely loved all of her grandchildren. Vivian kept us laughing as she would recount stories about absentminded things she would do. One time in particular, she was shopping and misplaced her glasses. She returned to the pharmacy counter to see if she had left them there. The clerk said, "No, I haven't seen them." After Vivian had given up the search and walked out to her car, she realized she was wearing them. She thoroughly enjoyed repeating that story and loved to laugh at herself. Unfortunately, a stroke has left her unable to speak for the most part. The whole family greatly misses being able to converse with her.

Jim's dad was the kindest man you could ever meet. Arnold was greatly respected by everyone who knew him, and each of his kids felt like the most special person on earth when they were with him. He was a hard worker, as one would have to be to raise such a large family, and was a World War II veteran. Arnold and his brother-in-law came from North Dakota to Montana to move a large historic home called the Greenough Mansion across a bridge to its new location. They cut the roof off and then cut the mansion into three more pieces so it could be hauled by semi-trucks over the river without being too heavy for the bridge. Once in its final place, it then had to be put back together. Since Montanans love to tell North Dakota jokes, he always enjoyed telling the story about how it took some North Dakotans to figure out how to move that structure.

After coming to the beautiful town of Missoula to complete the job, Jim's parents loved it so much they moved the family there. Jim was six years old at the time. Several years after we were married, the old Greenough Mansion, which was being used as a posh restaurant, burned to the ground. It was located on a hill overlooking the city, so everyone in town could observe its demise. I felt a bit sad that day reflecting on how, in a way, that home had brought my husband and I together. I wondered how many others' lives were in one way or another impacted by the beautiful old home.

Arnold had a wonderful sense of humor and would come up with some of the corniest jokes. I can still remember how he wore his baseball cap perched high on his head and that he loved to watch boxing on TV. Vivian called it "bang bang," motioning with her fists in the air. Arnold would make a face with his dentures just partway out, which made the grandkids laugh hysterically. He was a warm, loving father and grandfather, whom his adult children affectionately called "Daddy." Arnold made me feel loved and accepted, as though I were one of his own.

Early on in my dating relationship with Jim, I decided to call him at his house. I don't think I had ever called a guy before, so I was quite nervous. When I began to speak to Jim, the male voice on the other end of the line said, "This isn't Jim, this is his dad." I said, "No it's not, it's you." This went on for a bit until I realized I was indeed speaking with Arnold. He asked if I wanted to leave a message for Jim, but I felt so stupid. I said, "No thank you," and got off the phone as quickly as possible. Once I got to know Arnold better, he would tell that story and seemed to enjoy being mistaken for a younger man. Their voices really were similar, though.

One night Jim and I decided to go up to his parents' house to watch TV after we'd been out on a date for a while. Apparently Jim's dad had heard a noise but didn't realize it was us coming into the garage. He opened the door wide from the house into the garage, and all he had on was his underwear. Embarrassed, he quickly flung the door shut and went back to bed. I wanted to leave because I too was embarrassed and didn't know him very well at the time. Jim convinced me to come in, but of course there was no sign of Arnold, thankfully. That was another story that was funny later once we became better acquainted. That's the only time I ever saw him in his underwear, I am happy to say!

We had made a somewhat regular habit of going on vacation with Arnold and Vivian. They even purchased a minivan since they were always happy to cart their adult children and grandkids around. In the summer of 1998, Jim and I were planning to travel around Montana with the boys, tent-camping and going on hikes, for the most part. This wasn't a trip that was as conducive for his parents to go on as some others we had taken. I knew Vivian wouldn't want to sleep in a tent, but we were hoping to save money by not always staying in a hotel and our plans did not include areas where family lived. Neither Jim nor I could break it to them when Arnold asked, "Where are we going on vacation this year?" At first I was disappointed since we were unable to follow through with our original idea. His parents had a hard time keeping up while sightseeing with us, and especially with the boys, now that they were junior high and high school age. However, later in the year, I was especially thankful we went ahead and altered our plans to accommodate Jim's mom and dad.

Arnold was scheduled for heart surgery in November of 1998. He'd had other procedures done in the past, so I normally wouldn't have been terribly concerned about it, but this time he kept saying he was ready to go if the Lord wanted to take him. None of us liked the sound of that. His kids came home prior to the surgery to get family pictures done, but I noticed Arnold wasn't smiling like he usually did. No one really wanted to admit it, but I think everyone had the same thought in the back of their minds: "Just in case." The surgery turned out great, and Arnold looked very good. His coloring had changed from a pale grayish to quite rosy afterward. We all breathed a sigh of relief. I guess we had worried for nothing.

On Friday night, we went up to the hospital to visit Arnold, and he was teasing me, as he always did. It was good to see him feeling so much better since his Monday surgery, and he was scheduled to go home the next day. We left to watch our son play in his basketball game, feeling really at ease. No sooner were we seated in the bleachers than a police officer walked into the gym to find us. Even though the officer was a colleague of Jim's, I had a sinking feeling something was dreadfully wrong. Arnold had a stroke moments after we left, and it was critical. We were the last people to see that twinkle in his eyes and hear his last jokes. Jim's siblings rushed home, and the difficult decision was made to pull life support. Arnold got to go home after all, but it wasn't the home on Rattlesnake Drive. This pillar in the family, the gentle man with the big heart, was gone.

The memorial service was a wonderful tribute to a great man, but now we all had to get on with the business of living without him. One niece said she hadn't realized it before, but that "Grandpa was the glue that held this family together." The family was reeling after such a great loss. We were all still in disbelief, trying to carry on in life without the stabilizing force of Jim's dad. He had a way of managing everyone with such gentleness. Even a simple phrase like, "Oh, don't be so dumb," had a huge effect. Whoever needed to hear it could receive it from him and would quit being dumb! Jim's mom, after being married to him for so many years, was lost. One of our nieces and her family moved into the house with Vivian for a while, and then they bought it from her and she moved in with us.

I was very excited to have Vivian stay with us and was determined to make it as comfortable as I could for her. Jim's siblings had enjoyed coming home to see their parents in the past, so I assumed that would still be the case. His sisters were all tremendous hostesses, so I wanted to do everything just right. I was homeschooling my youngest son at the time, and Garrett was now attending a public high school. Since I had recently resigned from my teaching position, I had time to focus my attention on the home.

Planning for Vivian's move, Jim and I purchased a house that seemed better suited to accommodate our changing needs. While we were remodeling and Vivian was still living with her granddaughter up at her house, she began to share things with us about what our niece and her husband were doing. Vivian told us that she was being taken advantage of financially, as Vivian would purchase diapers for their child and never be reimbursed, for example. Both Jim and I were not very excited to hear of this, but then I stopped to think about it. This just didn't sound like our niece. I could see Vivian buying things for them because she enjoyed helping her kids and grandkids out, but I believed our niece had wonderful intentions while sharing a home with her grandma. When Jim described how he felt about what his mom had told him, I said, "Wait, honey, we need to be careful not to jump to conclusions." I am unsure exactly why Jim's mom felt a need to say these things, since it was obvious she loved our niece and her family. Knowing that Vivian would be living with us next was a sobering thought for me, because if she would say these things about her own flesh and blood, I might be in for big trouble. Understandably, having Arnold gone after virtually spending a lifetime with him seemed to put Vivian into a tail-spin that greatly affected the rest of the family for a period of time.

Once Vivian moved into our home, we returned to her church. This was an easy transition because it was very close to where we were now living, and it was the one Jim grew up in. Our furniture was moved to the basement, and we put hers in the living room, since I wanted Vivian to feel as comfortable as possible. In the back of my mind, I couldn't forget what had happened between Vivian and her granddaughter while they lived together, and they were blood relatives. What was going to happen now, in our home, since I was just a daughter-in-law? I decided

I would make sure there was nothing she could possibly complain to anyone about by being the perfect daughter-in-law. That should take care of it.

When the first relatives visited our home after Vivian moved in early that first autumn, I had a short-term falling out with one of Jim's sisters. I had been so focused on doing everything flawlessly—fixing a nice meal, having the house spotless, and generally being a good hostess—that something slipped by me. The second day our company was there, we all visited our niece up at Vivian's former home. By that time, I became aware that one of Jim's sisters, who lived nearby, was upset I hadn't invited her to dinner when our company first came. I'd always gotten along well with Jim's sister, but it hadn't even occurred to me to include her, since I was so busy attending to our guests' needs.

Generally, when family members visited prior to Arnold's death, everyone gathered up at their house for meals, but for some reason, it hadn't crossed my mind to invite others from the area. It is no wonder my sister-in-law felt slighted. She had obviously known of our plans for dinner and assumed things would be the same as before her father had passed away. I'm not quite sure how Jim's parents could afford to feed everyone all the time, but now everything was different. I did not intentionally mean to hurt anyone, so I immediately attempted to apologize when I saw her. She responded, "You *knew* I wanted to come to dinner." I then stated that I really had not even thought about it, and no one had mentioned it to me. She said, "Yes, you did know."

Okay, now I was being accused of lying, and that was a trigger for me. I completely blew up, trying to defend myself. Then I walked all the way home, approximately seven miles, stopping first at my sister's house. I was extremely upset because after working so hard to please Jim's mom and his family, I still found myself in hot water. At first I didn't want my husband to locate me on his drive home, so I took some side streets, but by the time I walked all that way and he hadn't even attempted to come to my rescue, I was a little hurt. Thankfully, it didn't take long to mend this with Jim's sister. We both realized we had overreacted, but I believed I had been the most emotional about it and felt pretty foolish afterward.

I thought everything was going extremely well between Jim's mom and me for quite a while after she moved in, but then we started hearing about matters Vivian had shared with family members. Apparently some things were bothering her, but instead of talking to us about them, she went to other people. Hearing of these things was extremely difficult for me since I had tried so hard to please her and the family. I had always desired to be closer to some of Jim's sisters, but now I feared many were believing I was not nice to their mother. If only they had known the truth.

Vivian kept telling us that she wanted to pay rent, and she continually asked us to tell her how much. It would have been reasonable to request some compensation, since we had so much more company to feed now that she lived with us, not to mention the increase in our mortgage and utilities. We ended up going through $5,000 of our savings while she lived with us in only thirteen and a half months. Twice, she gave us $250, which we did not even ask for, and she purchased some groceries on a couple of occasions. Some of the siblings thought we were charging her rent, and we found out through the grapevine that they were not happy about it. I believe they weren't aware of the true financial details of our situation or they wouldn't have been upset. Living with us was certainly much less expensive for her than if she were in an assisted living home or even having to pay rent for an apartment.

After Vivian had stayed with us about seven or eight months, there was one span of about forty days when we had company every day without a single day free. One couple would leave, I would wash the bedding, and the next would arrive. When Jim's mom decided to go to Spokane, Washington, to visit one of her daughters for Mother's Day, I thought it would be a nice opportunity to have my side of the family for dinner to celebrate with my own mom. I had not been able to do much with them for quite some time, since I was so preoccupied with changing sheets and cooking meals for Vivian's company. We decided to serve Sunday dinner buffet style on Mother's Day. Since I did not have much room on my countertops, Jim suggested I move a basket of Vivian's coffee supplies and her coffee maker to her dresser for the day. That seemed like a good idea, so I did. After my family left and I cleaned up the kitchen, I was very tired. I forgot to put her coffee things back on the counter before she returned home that night. Big mistake.

For the next several months, the coffee basket seemed to be all I heard about—through emails, at the mall, and someone even mentioned it to me at a friend's funeral. There was no escaping it. One of Vivian's best friends wouldn't even look at me when Jim and I ran into her while shopping. Previously she had always been friendly toward me. Vivian volunteered at the church office, folding and stuffing bulletins. Because of what I was constantly confronted with, I felt sure she must be telling the women in the office the same things. I got to the point where I didn't want to go anywhere, including church, since I thought everyone in the world must think I was the worst daughter-in-law ever. I no longer had work as an outlet, so I was feeling extremely isolated. There was no safe place for me where I felt accepted, not even in my own home.

When one of Jim's relatives came to visit, she was going to take Vivian shopping. Jim's mom struggled with a lot of fears and wouldn't go anywhere by herself after Arnold died, even during the day. This opportunity would allow me some time to do whatever I chose. I was very appreciative because I found myself attending many things, sometimes even the seniors' Bible study at church with Vivian, since she was hesitant to go alone. This would be a nice break. After sincerely offering my thanks, the family member responded with sarcasm, "Well, I thought this was your ministry." I was so taken aback, I had no response.

When I had resigned from teaching and told my coworkers that Jim's mom would be moving in with us, they signed a card with comments like, "God's blessings on you as you begin ministering to your mother-in-law." Jim had shown the card to his mother, and apparently she was offended by what they had written and proceeded to tell family members. I could not control what the teachers said, but I'm positive I would not have shown it to Vivian. I had a feeling it wouldn't sit well with her, but Jim hadn't thought about that. He shared it because he felt it was such a nice card. But now the damage was done, as evidenced by the comment from Jim's relative.

Later that summer, Jim's family was having a reunion. With all that had been happening, I really did not want to attend, but I knew he didn't want to miss it. Jim understood how difficult it would be for me, so he said we didn't have to go if I didn't want to. We ended up going because I chose to do so for my husband's sake. It was absolutely miserable for me. Since we had decided we were attending so late and there were no cabins left for us to rent, one of Jim's sisters offered their deck for us to sleep on. I was completely stressed out the entire time, imagining that many did not really want me there. I hardly slept a wink the whole weekend, and in the dark of night, my head was spinning and my heart felt ready to burst. It was a dreadful experience, one I was relieved to be done with.

As difficult as this period of time was for me, it may have been even harder on Jim. I wanted him to talk to his mom about everything because I didn't feel at ease, since I was the daughter-in-law. He was in a tough position, and I felt sorry for him. It can be hard having the two most important women in your life living in the same house when there is trouble brewing.

Jim reverted back to his old way of handling things, and that was to try to ignore it. Unfortunately, this was not going to go away by itself. I wish I had been well mentally during this time period, because I would have had the confidence to handle it much differently than I did. I felt attacked, and therefore I assumed the victim role, as I had in the past. Jim tried to cover for his mom, which greatly disappointed me. I know he was simply trying to do damage control, but it didn't feel good at the time because I wanted him to defend me. My biggest problem was I worried so much about pleasing people, particularly his family, that I forgot about pleasing God. I wanted his family's approval in the worst way, but it didn't seem possible for me to obtain it. Jim ended up going on blood pressure medication. By this it became obvious he wasn't truly able to ignore what was going on.

Another way Jim attempted to escape the drama in our house was to spend a lot of time talking to and helping a friend of his around her house. This was a nurse he'd met many years earlier through numerous trips to the emergency room with people in his custody. She was older than we were, and I had never felt threatened by their relationship, even though there had been a difficult situation involving her years earlier.

Jim had a cell phone he took to work with him, but I paid all the bills. I never looked at any of the numbers he was calling until I received a bill that was exorbitantly high. We could not afford this, so I checked to see why it had increased so much. I noticed that he was calling this friend during daytime hours, and we were being charged for all of those minutes. I mentioned it to Jim and suggested that he limit his cell phone use to evening and night time minutes. He agreed. A while later, the same thing happened, so I looked over the bill again. I noticed that Jim was calling her number, but the call only lasted one minute each time. Then the next minute, without fail, it listed an incoming call from an unknown number that lasted many minutes, or even more than an hour. It was pretty easy to figure out that he was calling her and telling her to call him right back. This seemed a bit deceptive to me, so I asked him about it. Eventually he realized I knew what was up, and I told him I didn't care if he talked to her; I just didn't want it to cause us to have a bill we couldn't afford.

I believed she was not the type of person he would be interested in beyond friendship, as she was more like a big sister to him. It became clear through a series of events while Vivian lived with us that this was not a healthy thing to be involved in, but Jim couldn't see it at first. His friend loved to give gifts to Jim and our sons, but she didn't seem to like me very much. One day he drove her and one of her friends to a town two hours away to go to the trial of the person who had shot the police officer. On this trip, she did actually buy me a gift, an expensive box of chocolates. I was prone to migraine headaches, especially if I consumed too much chocolate. Unknowingly on her part, this probably wasn't the best gift for me. I did overindulge, and as a result, I suffered from a migraine, so the only present I can say she's ever given me is a massive headache! Jim and his friend were spending more and more time together as I was feeling more and more alone in a home that felt like there was a dark raincloud hovering within its walls.

After his friend was injured in a car wreck, he began helping her around the house even more. Jim told me he would like it if I would try to become her friend too. Her home was filthy and smelled heavily of cigarette smoke and animal urine. Part of her carpet had been torn up in the corner because her pets used that area as a litter box. In spite of all that, I attempted to befriend her. She had a difficult time moving about due to her injuries, so when we went to visit her with our boys, she was sitting in a chair with her nightie on. It was not completely see-through but nearly, and she had nothing to cover with. I could hardly look at her since her massive, unbridled breasts would move to and fro every time she lifted one of her arms.

After we returned home and the boys were no longer within earshot, I spoke with Jim about my concerns. I certainly didn't think it was appropriate for our adolescent sons to be exposed to that, not to mention Jim. He said he hadn't noticed. Oh please! There was no way anyone could miss that. Finally, Jim told me he would talk to her about it. Well, that's not what I desired; I didn't want Jim to go back there at all, especially by himself. The very next day, Jim told me he had spoken with her and she agreed to cover herself the next time we came over. I was supposed to go in first to get her a blanket and then Jim could enter. I was not happy at all that they felt so comfortable talking about her breasts. It seemed too familiar, in my opinion, but his comfort level was probably due to being raised with seven girls.

In spite of my misgivings, I agreed to try once again. I entered her home first, as planned, and stood there for a while, not seeing any blankets in the room. Making small talk was so awkward that I couldn't bring myself to ask her where the blanket was, and she didn't offer. Eventually I gave up, moved to the doorway, and waved Jim in. This was one of the most uncomfortable evenings I've ever experienced. On our way home, Jim asked me why I hadn't covered her with a blanket, so I explained the reason. The next day, when they spoke, she told him it was her house and she didn't have to cover herself if she didn't want to. Apparently she had no intention of abiding by his request. My feeling was that if his friend was going to have that attitude, then she should expect to spend a lot of time alone. Obviously she did not care whether I was comfortable in her home. I requested that Jim quit visiting her, but that didn't happen yet.

During this period, Jim suggested I have breast implant surgery. He told me he wanted it for me, but this had to be the worst timing ever to bring something like this up. I had considered plastic surgery in the past due to the teasing I endured in junior high but was trying to accept myself the way God made me—that is, until I was reminded again. I made an appointment with a plastic surgeon, but I just couldn't follow through with it. The doctor told me he couldn't guarantee I wouldn't be a D cup after it was done. I still wanted to be able to run, and I wasn't ready to take a chance on being that large. I certainly didn't want to be Barbie. I just wanted to be normal. I thought about some of the women friends I had who were also smaller in size. They were attractive both inside and out. I remember watching the National Track and Field Championships on TV that summer, and I felt like the female runners had such beautiful, fit bodies, yet they did not have large breasts. Why couldn't I see myself how I viewed these other women?

One night, after the boys and Vivian had gone to their rooms, Jim was on the phone in the living room with this same friend. He had been talking to her for a very long time, and I was craving some attention from him. I decided to flash him so he would know to come to bed. He raised his eyebrows and gave me a nod, acknowledging that he had seen me. I thought he understood what I wanted, so I went to the bedroom, waiting for him. The next thing I knew, I heard the front door close. I put my bathrobe on and went out to the living room. Jim had just left to go visit her. My spirit was so deflated. It doesn't take too much imagination to figure out that my mind went wild. I was already feeling lonely, attacked, unappreciated, and deserted, so I didn't need to feel all of the old insecurity and trust issues flooding back. Talk about triggers for a manic episode.

As I think back to that time, I realize Jim was continually under pressure from me for years. Due to my own insecurity, I constantly watched where his eyes were directed as we passed grocery store magazines covered with scantily clad women. He made a point to turn away if we were watching television when an attractive woman came on the screen, as instantly, my piercing gaze was directed at him. In retrospect, it's no wonder he would suggest breast augmentation. Of course, I understand that men are extremely visual creatures and are drawn to attractive women, but I assumed the suggestion was because he was displeased with me, not that he might be weary of my intense scrutiny.

Sometime during mid to late summer, I started pressuring Jim more aggressively to speak with his mom. I felt I had been hung out for the wolves and was nearly ready to leave the home for a while until he could figure out who he was married to. Was our relationship valuable enough for him to stand up for me when he knew the truth about what was occurring? Whenever I would bring up anything concerning our situation with his mom, I was determined to remain calm and steadfast.

Early in our relationship, on a few occasions when we were arguing, Jim hit the side of his pickup with his fist. It had worked to get me to shut up. After so many years without having things escalate to that point, here we were again. I brought up the subject of what was going on with his mom and told him that we needed to deal with it. One time he punched the dresser I was leaning on. Another time, he punched the pillow my head was resting on. I decided I didn't even care if he hit me; I was no longer going to stay quiet. Intimidation would not work this time. After all, being hurt physically would seem like nothing compared to the emotional pain I was experiencing. Jim never did hit me, and taking a stand actually worked. He finally decided to address the issue with his mom.

Vivian lived with us about one year before Jim spoke with her about what was taking place. He tried to impress upon her the need to come to us if something was bothering her rather than going to other family members. This conversation did not go well at all, basically for one reason. Out of frustration, I jumped into the middle of it since I thought he wasn't doing an adequate job defending me. After an entire year of trying to be the good daughter-in-law and keeping my mouth shut, I couldn't seem to stay quiet any longer.

As Jim was speaking with her in her bedroom, I walked down the hall to get ready for bed. I overheard his mom say, "But she moved my basket." His response was a very sympathetic, "I know." That was it! I'd had enough. He seemed to be coddling her on this issue, and I was fed up to my eyeballs about that stupid coffee basket! I burst into the doorway, and said, "About the basket . . ." A heated discussion ensued between Vivian and me about what had taken place, and it was terribly upsetting for both of us. In retrospect, I wasn't even angry at Vivian but

116

actually at Jim for not sticking up for me the way I wanted him to. I wish I had not become involved in that conversation at all. At the very least, I should have directed my disappointment toward him.

I was sorry I had not allowed Jim to address this in his own way, because unfortunately, Vivian ended up moving out of our house to live with one of her daughters about a month later. One of Jim's sisters was visiting when the confrontation occurred, and I felt so badly afterward. Now I was afraid she would believe I had been mistreating her mother; after all, there was the proof. Thankfully, it turned out that she was able to see past it and still loved me.

As I reflect back on all the years I've known Vivian, sometimes I feel bad for her. She has been a wonderful mother and person, but I don't know if she always believed that herself. Now as I think of the coffee basket incident, I wonder if those objects didn't represent something deeper for Vivian. Maybe the fact that they were unwanted, though only for a day, made her feel unwanted on some level as well. After all, she had been uprooted from her home after Arnold's death, and everything in her life had changed. I wish she could have recognized the great love I had for her. Maybe that's part of the reason what transpired while she lived with us hurt us both as much as it did. We were desiring love and acceptance but never fully felt we obtained it, even though it was right there all along. Insecurity can certainly cause a person to think and act in wrong ways. I know this all too well.

If only Jim and I had been mature enough to have handled this situation differently, there may have been a better outcome. Jim could have gently addressed issues as soon as they came up rather than trying to escape. I wish I'd had the confidence to keep from becoming defensive and taking things personally, because I knew I'd done my best to take care of his mother. It required a bit of time for my relationships in the family to fully heal after this, but I really do love Jim's family. I am also incredibly grateful for their forgiveness and love and that I am part of such a wonderful group of people. We all need a little forgiveness once in a while.

"For if you forgive men when they sin against you, your heavenly Father will also forgive you. But if you do not forgive men their sins, your Father will not forgive your sins" (Matt. 6:14–15).

CHAPTER 12

ESCAPE

And God is faithful: he will not let you be tempted beyond what you can bear. But when you are tempted, he will also provide a way out so that you can stand up under it.

—1 Corinthians 10:13b

I was in terrible shape after the events of the past several years: weary of pressure, weary of people and relationships, and weary of hurting all the time. Jim and I had some friends who lived on a mountain and had to snowmobile to their house in the winter. I was enamored with the apparent simplicity of their lifestyle. After convincing Jim, we finally found twenty-six acres for sale in our friends' neighborhood and made plans to move up there. Garrett was in college by this time, so he stayed with my parents for a while and then moved into a fraternity until he graduated. I was still homeschooling Chad, who was now a sophomore in high school.

Life was not always easy up on the mountain, but it certainly was an adventure. The first summer, after moving most of our things into storage, we had to put up enough firewood for the winter, drill a well, and get the house enclosed. We purchased a camp trailer and stayed in it from June until about October. We kept one small TV and a few videos that were leftover from packing in the shed next to the camper. Chad got so desperate for something to watch that he was willing to sit through *Old Yeller* and *The Sound of Music* with me. Other than that, we spent our spare time hiking with the dogs, shooting a compound bow and guns at targets, and eventually stocking up on items from the store for the long winter.

Future home site on the mountain, with a spectacular view.

Jim and I were novices at collecting firewood, but we went out and did our best. One day, the chainsaw slipped and Jim ended up slicing through his jeans to the kneecap. We were unable to see how bad it was due to his pants covering the wound, so we took off for the emergency room at the hospital in Missoula. I was driving and asked him how he was doing. He said he didn't think it was too bad and it wasn't bleeding much. When we arrived at the ER, we decided that I would drop him off to go look for some loggers chaps, since we would be out there many more times before we were finished. It would be much safer having his legs covered in leather.

There were people near the entrance to the ER, and when I let Jim out of the truck to walk in, I noticed there was actually quite a bit of blood on the back of his pants. I hollered out to him, "Don't get blood on the chair!" I realized how that must have sounded to the bystanders, but I was concerned that he wouldn't realize until he got up that he had stained a chair. After all, I was simply trying to alleviate an embarrassing situation for him, but in so doing, I embarrassed myself! When I returned to the hospital without chaps, Jim asked me why I hadn't purchased any. I said, "They didn't have the right kind, and they were too expensive." The doctor jokingly said, "Oh, he's not worth it, huh?" That's not really what I meant, but we've laughed about that many times since.

We were attempting to build our home debt-free, so we lived in it when it was very unfinished. The shell was there, with yellow, plastic-covered insulation for exterior walls. The job of insulating the ceiling was extremely difficult, and it felt like I was climbing up and down a jungle gym all day long. The itchy fiberglass insulation just about drove me crazy, since I had to drape it over my shoulder every time I carried a new piece up the three sets of scaffolding. I finally completed that job and laundered the clothing I had worn. Naively, I decided to wear the same clothes to town one day, and the longer I was in them, the itchier I felt. The fiberglass was not all removed from my clothes during washing. I was going berserk until I finally decided I needed to buy a new outfit, since it was implausible to drive all the way home to change.

Jim was at work one day when I was charged with stapling the plastic up on the ceilings and walls. It was October, and the air was crisp. I could not start a fire in the wood stove until this job was completed, since the plastic would have melted to it if it were to make contact. Our ceiling was twenty-four feet high, so I had to climb up on the scaffolding in order to reach the top, and I am not terribly fond of being that high. Working alone with long sheets of plastic was difficult, to say the least, and I had become discouraged. I was nearly ready to give up and start a fire, since the chill in the house was very uncomfortable. As a last-ditch effort, I prayed that God would send someone to help me since I knew Jim would be disappointed if I didn't get this done. Just before giving in to start the fire to warm the house, our pastor, who does construction work on the side, came up for a visit. I asked if he would be willing to help me staple the plastic to the ceiling. Then a short while later, a neighbor who also works in construction came over to see if I needed any help. This was such a wonderful answer to prayer, since they completed it without my assistance. I was so thankful I didn't have to climb up there for this particular job again.

Our bedroom was only framed up, but the bathroom was sheet-rocked for privacy. Not having any kitchen cabinets presented a challenge, but somehow we managed. Finally, after two years, we decided to borrow the money to finish the house. It turned out great! We had our beautiful home in the woods with knotty-pine cabinets and a wonderfully, massive log railing that I sanded and finished myself. We felt a lot of pride after having worked so hard on our home.

Though the land was inexpensive, finishing the home cost more than we had budgeted. We didn't realize how much we would be investing in a well but knew it would be important to find water way up there before breaking ground. We were fairly confident since our neighbor's wells were only around one hundred feet deep, which is surprising since some people in the valley below have wells at up to six hundred feet in depth. We did not strike water the first day of drilling, and a depth of over two hundred feet had been reached. Since we had already sold our house in town and were living in our camp trailer, this was cause for concern. After the well-driller left that evening, we prayed for water from the rock beneath. Touching a long stick to the site, remembering the story of Moses and the Israelites as they wandered in the desert with no water, we prayed. God had told Moses to strike the rock at Horeb with his staff and water would come out for the people to drink. If it worked for them, maybe it would work for us. The next day, the driller quickly hit water, and we had a well at 225 feet.

Probably among the most costly nonbudgeted items were the power system and snowmobile expense. We were a bit naive when it came to those prior to moving there. Living off the power grid is a way of life with many choices. Not having had experience with it before, we began making decisions based on how much it would cost to install things rather than long-range planning. Our power system was adequate, however, and once we grew accustomed to it, it seemed normal to us. The end result was that anyone visiting us would not even realize we were living off-grid unless they stayed long enough for the generator to come on. We had an inverter and battery bank for power storage. I usually ran the generator in the evening when it was dark so we would not have to conserve on lights while I vacuumed, did laundry, filled the pressure tank, and charged up the batteries for the next day's use. We had satellite TV, so we didn't really feel like we were doing without any comforts. Chad had restrictions on energy use, so he watched TV and worked on the computer when the generator was running as well. Cell phones were a lifesaver since there were no land lines up there. and thank goodness for propane appliances.

When we bought our snowmobiles, we didn't know too much about them since neither one of us had ever owned one before. The two previously owned trail machines we purchased were adequate for our needs but were not fun to play on. They each had two seats. so we thought that was enough for us—at least until we rode them. We are tall people, and it was hard for us to double up on them all the time. not to mention if one of them broke down, which they do occasionally. we would be in bad shape. In January we purchased a brand new. faster sled for Jim to ride since he had to go to work each day. It was nice to have the trail sleds, too, for when we brought company home with us.

I was feeling a little bit guilty the first time Jim had to ride a snowmobile to get to work, since it had been my idea to move up there. He had to leave before 6:00 a.m. while it was still cold and dark. and I hopped back into my warm bed after stoking the wood stove. I prayed that somehow the ride down to the bottom would be fun and memorable for Jim. I admit it was kind of a selfish prayer to relieve my guilt. He called me on his way driving in and said excitedly, "You're not going to believe what I saw when I was going down the mountain this morning!" He told me he had seen a whole herd of elk crossing the road and had to stop quickly to avoid hitting them. It made his day and mine both. Thank You, Lord, for the little blessings.

We purchased a trailer to pull behind the snowmobiles so we could bring home groceries and fuel. It's funny to think back now about all the tricks we learned in order to transport items home. My friend had told me no matter how she wrapped eggs, she had never gotten a complete dozen home unbroken. Jim suggested I wear a backpack to put them in so I would absorb more of the shock. Funny how he thought *I* should be the one to wear the backpack! I was envisioning myself with eggs running down my back by the time we got home. Well, it turned out to be a great idea. I never broke one single egg while we lived up there.

One of our neighbors raised chickens so she didn't have to worry about transporting eggs. The only problem then was that they had to worry about predators. A bear broke into the chicken feed. even though the shed door was locked. On another occasion, their chickens began disappearing one at a time. Eventually they realized that a badger was dining on the chickens, and he had made a den underneath the house. The owner piled rocks at the entrance to the den, but the animal used its powerful claws to quickly dig a new one. Apparently it had become accustomed to its badger bed and breakfast and did not want to leave quite yet.

There was one time, before we really knew how to secure our groceries, when we were missing several items by the time we arrived home. As we backtracked, we found fruit, vegetables, lunch meat, exploded yogurt cups, cottage cheese, and a loaf of bread that had been run over by a snowmobile. I'm not really sure what happened to the bananas, though. Some of the items were still in good condition, but we learned to put to use lots of bins and straps after that.

A trip to town was quite an event for me. I had a history of being fearful of icy roads ever since I was a senior in high school, when I lost control of my car on a hill. The vehicle turned completely around, so I was traveling down backward, narrowly missing two other cars that had come to a stop on the side of the road. Making the commute from on top of a mountain and then driving on a two-lane, winding highway challenged me immensely. Though I trust Jim's driving abilities, I am afraid of others', so my stress when he was at the wheel routinely caused a heated disagreement. I was jumpy, rubbed my legs, pressed on an imaginary brake, and let out noises and gasps when I became nervous. It drove him nearly as crazy as I was acting!

Living up there was actually good for me because I had to face my fears quite often, but the bad roads were not so good for our relationship. One time, I actually threatened to jump out of the moving vehicle as I was screaming, which really makes no sense, since tumbling on the pavement would definitely do some damage. The funny thing is, I trusted Jim's driving more than my own, but at the same time, I had difficulty when I was not in control. Though much improved, this is something I still struggle with at times. Thankfully, Jim has become incredibly patient concerning this.

Because I was homeschooling and rarely employed during this period of time, I either stayed home or went to town for the entire day to run all of my errands. It took a total of forty-five minutes to travel home in the winter between driving on the highway and then trekking up the mountain on a snowmobile. We always had so many things to remember to bring. A flashlight was one of them.

Our neighbors had returned from town at about the same time one evening, so I was distracted by visiting with them. As I transferred all of my purchases to the trailer, the baskets on the sleds, and the backpack, my dog, Max, must have been off marking a tree or something. I forgot to scan the area with my flashlight for the little lap dog I'd brought along that day. He usually went with us and would ride right ahead of me on my seat, with his front legs on the gas tank. Max always knew when we were going to town, and I didn't have the heart to leave him home, so on went the little doggy sweater.

Well, this night, I made it all the way home on my snowmobile before I realized I had left him at the bottom of the mountain, five miles away. I panicked and took off on my snowmobile, feeling sick. What if he wandered off and got lost in the dark, or worse yet, was eaten by a mountain lion? I would never forgive myself. Partway down the mountain, I met my neighbor, and there sat Max between his legs on the snowmobile. What a relief! I made sure that never happened again.

After living up there for a few years, we went through a stretch of time where everything seemed to go wrong. We were wondering if our pump had gone out on our well or maybe even the well had gone dry since we couldn't get any water. In actuality, it was caused by the wrong wires being connected when we were trying to fix our generator, since it also kept having problems. It is hard to get by without both power and water. After spending a lot of money trying to fix the generator, we finally bought a new one.

We had a couple of friends looking at the pump issue when another neighbor drove up in our truck. He had borrowed it to get firewood and brought it back after dropping a tree on the box of the truck. When he and his wife got out of the truck and approached us, they looked more than a bit nervous. Jim and I started laughing. After all, what else can you do when it seems like everything is going wrong? Needless to say, they were both surprised and relieved at our reaction. After hearing what happened, we were glad it wasn't worse. The neighbor had his kids with him when he was out cutting down trees, and there was also a trailer behind for firewood. Two of the kids were in the cab of the truck, while the third was standing in the trailer. The tree fell between the children to hit the bed of the pickup. We were so thankful, since a truck is replaceable but children are not. Our neighbors found another box for the truck, but it was a different color. Now our son owns the vehicle, and it is a one-of-a-kind.

In addition to my little lap dog, Max, I owned two rottweilers before we moved up there. Jim had named our female Babe to try to take my mind off having any more children. We bred her once and kept one male pup out of the litter. His name was Jake. When he was a little puppy, we allowed them in the house once in a while, and Jake would run to Chad when he was practicing his trumpet. Sitting right in front of Chad, he would howl at the bell of the trumpet, and then Babe would join in. It was the funniest thing. I figured it must not hurt his ears or he wouldn't run toward the noise. Then I began making trumpet-like sounds with my mouth, and I could get the same reaction. They both loved to lean into your leg, constantly touching. When he got older, I bought Jake a typical tough dog collar with metal spikes. This did not work out so well. Whenever I went outside to see the dogs, he would run toward me, doing figure eights around my legs. I am tall, but he was too tall, especially in the summer, because he would scratch up my bare thighs with his collar. That collar ended up in a garage sale, and a kid with black clothes and lots of piercings purchased it.

The rottweilers had not been full-time house dogs until we moved up on the mountain, and my huge 125-pound male became more protective. Jake seemed to react more aggressively if a person had at least three of the following four traits. He did not like males, people with some sort of face covering like facial hair or a snowmobile helmet, if they were nervous and acted afraid of him, or if they were inside our house. He bit one neighbor and left a nick on his hand. The dogs figured out how to lift the latch on the kennel while we were gone one day, so this person put them back in for us. We took better care to secure the kennel after that because we did not want to take any chances on something bad happening while we were away for the day.

Another male neighbor came over to visit inside our house, and though he attempted to make friends with Jake, he was visibly nervous around him. That seemed to be a huge trigger for him, so he lunged at the man and bit him on the leg before Jim grabbed Jake and held him back. Thank goodness this man had heavy work pants on, so the result was only a bruised thigh. Jake also had an injured leg, which caused him pain whenever we took him hiking, so we considered surgery. Already knowing in my heart what the verdict would be, I called my veterinarian about the problems we were experiencing. She advised that we put him down due to a combination of the injury and the increasingly aggressive behavior.

Ending my dog's life was one of the hardest things I've ever had to do, especially since it wasn't due to old age or illness. His offense was that he loved me too much and wanted to protect me. Taking him to the vet caused me to feel like I was betraying him and his loyalty. He had no idea I was leading him to his death. If only I could have explained to him what I wanted him to do so he would understand. I kept remembering newspaper articles I'd read about dogs who had severely mauled or killed someone after they had a history of biting, and I knew I couldn't live with myself if that were to happen. Now I understood why people had so much difficulty with such a decision. My veterinarian had a little struggle getting the needle in the first time, and I had to hold Jake still. Could we somehow not have to do this? As Jake finally drifted off after the second attempt, my eyes were blurred as tears were rolling down my cheeks.

I went home to Babe, my other rottweiler, who was Jake's mother. She knew something was terribly wrong when I didn't return with Jake. Babe was as depressed as I, and we seemed to feed off of each other's emotions. Whenever I took Babe out to go to the bathroom, she would hide under a brush pile and had to be coaxed out. I spent the next three days or so in bed. I could barely stand to watch Jake's mother grieving, and I felt guilty. I bought a new female golden retriever puppy to try to take our minds off our loss. Babe developed cancer shortly thereafter and died at the age of eight. A week after her death, I purchased a male golden retriever puppy so we could breed the two golden retrievers later on. The new puppies definitely helped alleviate some of the pain of losing my rottweilers, and they were certainly not a threat to our neighbors, but I still missed my other dogs.

Hiking up the Garnet Range Road with Chad and the dogs.

Jim had always felt good about having Jake up there when he worked nights since no one in their right mind would try to enter the house with a massive rottweiler head staring through the window at them. One night, when I still had Babe and Jake, we had a couple of drunk guys stop by. The gate at the bottom of the mountain was already locked for the winter, so the road was intended for snowmobile use only. How in the world had they driven in? The old county road was impassible, I was certain, at least for driving up. I stepped outside to speak with them while Chad was inside with the dogs, ready to help me if I needed it. Apparently they had come up from the other side of the mountain, thinking it would be a shortcut to get where they were attempting to go. The men had driven all the way down the mountain on our side to the gate but couldn't get through. Remembering our house lights, they returned for directions. I told them how they might be able to get out by an alternate route and was relieved when they left and didn't return.

We observed the most amazing wildlife while living up there. We saw a lynx cross our property once, numerous black bears, deer, elk, one mountain lion, rabbits, a badger, coyotes, owls, birds of all kinds, and even a moose and her calf. I was hiking with the dogs when I saw the moose. Out of all the animals listed, that is probably the most dangerous, especially a cow with her calf. Thank goodness I grabbed my dogs and leashed them before they noticed her, or I'm afraid they would have run up to her. Then I might have been in trouble, since she would have chased them to protect her baby, and of course they would come back to me. The dogs are definitely faster than I am, and I did not want to have my hands full with an angry moose.

An owl tried to catch one of our cats, and as the cat flipped on her back to protect herself, the owl sliced her belly open. She had a nasty gash all the way across, requiring a drain and numerous stitches. This particular cat was a great huntress herself, catching and killing everything from the smallest mice and birds to rabbits that were at least her size. We tried putting a bell on her, but it didn't phase her. Plus we became nervous that she would become the hunted, so we took the bell off since it wasn't accomplishing its intended purpose.

One night, around eleven o'clock, Chad and I heard a strange noise off in the distance. It didn't sound like a coyote, but it was definitely canine. The closer it came, we realized it might be a puppy howling. I began calling for it, and it came up the hill from the main road to our house. I'd never seen a dog quite like this. Its markings were like a beagle, but its ears were quite a bit longer, and it seemed a bit leggy for a beagle. Boy could it howl like one, though! She was an adorable little girl, definitely in the hound dog family, so we put an ad in the newspaper to see if we could find her owner. Surely someone would be missing her. Another person called and said that he had just lost his dog and wondered if we would give her to him if the owner did not turn up. He seemed like a really nice man, so we agreed.

After more than a week, we decided the owner was not going to show up, so the next day we would turn the dog over to the man who called about her. That night, we finally received a phone call. The puppy's owner had been out of town when she had escaped from her pen with another dog. The person taking care of the dogs didn't know what to do when one dog turned up without the other one. These were Walker Coonhounds, and this pup had traveled many miles to get to our house from where they lived in the valley. Apparently the dogs had followed a scent, and the younger one had become separated from the older dog. The owner was happy to have her returned, but we had to break the news to the nice gentleman who was expecting to receive his puppy the next day.

Living up there was a memorable experience. It was therapeutic in so many ways because I had time to go hiking, mountain biking, cross country skiing right from my doorstep, and snowmobiling, and I also did a lot of reading and cooking. It was a much slower pace, which was just what I seemed to need. However, I still had symptoms of this illness. Somehow it found me, even on the mountain.

There were actually other neighbors, beside our good friends, who were crazy enough to live way up there. Overall, we got along great and even had neighborhood dinner parties. There's nothing more amusing than seeing all of your guests ride up on snowmobiles. It highlighted the interesting lifestyle we'd chosen. We were there to assist each other if someone broke down or was out of something needed for baking. After all, it wasn't like there was a store around the corner.

Even the best relationships have their moments, however. Looking back, I can see that bipolar disorder was still an issue for me at the time, even though my stress level had been greatly reduced. One example was a difference of opinion over a dog issue with a friend. Their two dogs, including one that was 150 pounds, were allowed to roam the neighborhood causing trouble, and I let it bother me too much. Their larger dog would routinely pin one of my fifty-pound young golden retrievers down by the neck when he was on our property. My friend's attitude was that the dogs just needed to work it out. I wondered if she would have felt the same if I sent my teenage son over to put the hurt on her preschool-aged boy on their land every day. Somehow I didn't think she would feel the boys would need to work it out. I felt like I could hardly go outside on my own twenty-six acres with my dogs without fear of being ambushed.

After around three months of being paranoid every time I opened the door to take my dogs hiking or just to work on our property, Jim finally got to see what I'd been telling him about. He never seemed to really understand until he had to throw a chunk of wood at their dog to get it off of ours and chase it away. One time I even strained my hamstring trying to get my three dogs inside the house while keeping hers out. Jim and I finally had a talk with both the husband and wife about the issue since I figured if they knew what was happening, they would feel bad and fix the problem. Unfortunately, our friendship was pretty much ruined. The wife's angry response was, "But what am I supposed to do with the dogs while I homeschool?" You know, that was really not my problem, but I didn't say that. I had been patient and chose my words very carefully. She seemed like such a reasonable person, so I thought it would turn out much differently. Her icy reaction hurt my feelings because I thought I should be more important than an animal to her. I love my dogs, but I would never want their behaviors to inconvenience anyone else. They are my responsibility. Many of my inner conflicts were kept to myself, but sometimes my poor husband had to listen to me talk about things until he probably wished his ears would fall off. This was one of those occasions.

Certainly one of my greatest struggles while living up there happened because of my reaction to a birthday present. Jim, with the best of intentions, had purchased a massage gift certificate for me from a younger gal who always came out to talk to him when he was working traffic from the alley by her house. He had his favorite locations to catch people speeding and had also shown this spot to another officer he'd trained. This woman, whom Jim said looked similar to me, made a habit of approaching the other officer every time he worked that area too. It seemed to me she might have a thing for a man in a uniform, and I did not like it one bit.

For some reason, I had grown suspicious of this situation, which is silly since Jim would not have purchased a massage for me from someone if he was having an affair with her. Regardless, I mentioned it to a friend who had ridden as a citizen observer with my husband while he was on duty. The friend asked me if it was a particular location, and I said it was. This person then went on to tell me that Jim had taken him there and talked about this woman. My husband admitted something to him he hadn't revealed to me. Jim thought she might have a thing for cops too but said, "I don't know what she would see in an old guy like me, though."

I was livid! Did he *want* her to see something in him? I went totally out of control when I saw Jim. I grabbed a really cute, expensive figurine of a cop giving a teddy bear to a little girl, which his nurse friend from the emergency room had given him. Then I marched outside and smashed it on the sidewalk by our house. I'd had enough of these other women who were after my husband! I was so angry at him for continuing to go there to do traffic. My mind was conjuring up all kinds of possibilities. Now, when I look back, I feel so sorry for that poor man. He was just trying to do his job. I can't say I wouldn't be flattered if someone younger noticed me too, but it doesn't mean you are having an affair. I was certain he was at the time, though.

While still upset, I didn't even want to redeem the gift certificate, but I couldn't see wasting the money either. Besides, it had been forever since I'd had a massage, and it would allow me to see my competition. So I scheduled it and had a plan of attack in place too. As she was giving me my massage, I did quite a bit of talking. I told her how cops *rarely* leave their wives for other women. For some of them, if they do have an affair, it is just another notch in their belt. I also told her their routine joke about how if a woman wants to sleep with a uniform, just make sure it's been dry-cleaned before they return it. Crazy? Yes, but it gave me a lot of satisfaction, and it also worked. She never went out to visit with him after that and actually got back together with her boyfriend. Sometimes you've got to protect what belongs to you!

Being married to a police officer can be extremely challenging. Not only do other women become enamored with a man in uniform, but other difficulties can also arise. Throughout the years, we had our struggles due to his strange schedule. I frequently felt the responsibilities of the home and parenting fall squarely on my shoulders in his absence. He could not attend church for long periods of time, so I often assumed the role of spiritual leader in the home as I would get the boys to church services and other activities and would read Bible stories to them. He had to deal with some things on the job that I wasn't always crazy about either.

One Halloween I decided to ride with him as a citizen observer, and he pulled a truck over for a traffic violation. The next thing I knew, he returned without giving the driver a ticket. I asked why he let the person go. He explained that the young woman couldn't find her driver's license because her costume was her bra and panties, so she had nowhere to put it. Due to my insecurities, I wondered if he wouldn't have lingered on that call if I hadn't been with him. Jim also told me once that when they were assigned to walk the beat on weekend nights, they had to patrol through a strip club that used to be located downtown. I *hated* it when he had to walk the beat and often wondered what really happened when the officers were in there. Were they looking for trouble in the crowd, or did they stay a while to watch the show? I was so relieved when the place went out of business. I'm sure Jim's choice of profession affected me much more because of my bipolar disorder than it would have otherwise, as I sometimes obsessed about what he was seeing and doing on the job.

Absolutely the worst thing that happened during our mountaintop adventure totally blindsided me. I had become a reserve deputy a few years earlier and was required to ride along with a full-time deputy for training purposes. While I was out on patrol for the day, we were contacted over the radio with a message to call my husband right away. The full-time officer and I were in an area where cell phones didn't work, so we hurried to the nearest establishment to make the call. What Jim told me made me feel like someone punched me as hard as they could in the stomach. Feeling as though I might throw up, I started wailing, "No! No! No!" My precious nephew, Jeremy, had committed suicide. I guess we were both escaping our pain at that time, only in different ways.

CHAPTER 13

BACK TO REALITY

The Lord himself goes before you and will be with you;
he will never leave you nor forsake you. Do not be afraid;
do not be discouraged.

—Deuteronomy 31:8

After four years of life on the mountain, Jim was offered a change in his duties as a police officer. He became the school resource officer at the high school he graduated from. This was a very exciting opportunity, one he was perfectly suited to. Kids love him, and he genuinely cares about them. It gives the students an opportunity to see a cop as a real person, not just some authority figure who is trying to ruin their fun. The only problem was that, instead of working four ten-hour days, he would work Monday through Friday. In addition, there would be games, dances, open houses, and bonfires to attend. Chad had decided to move out of our house a few months prior to the news of this change, and our good friends had embarked on a singing ministry and so were rarely home. My last puppy in a litter of golden retrievers had recently been sold after I'd already started calling him by name, and I feared loneliness would set in for me. With mixed feelings, we made the decision to move back to civilization.

While living on the mountain, we started going to a little church in the valley below. We wanted to get to know people in the area rather than drive all the way in to town to worship. Because of the relationships we'd formed there, we were hoping to buy a home closer to town yet still far enough out to maintain our involvement in the church. Jim was a board member, and we were both youth group leaders.

As our search for a new home began, we became a bit discouraged. We were having difficulty finding anything available in our price range in the desired area. Finally, we gave up on locating a house out of town because we had already sold our home and needed to find something soon. We started going to open houses in Missoula. There was one being held in the neighborhood we had moved from four years earlier only a few doors down from our old house. Out of curiosity, one of our former neighbors came by to take a peek at it while we happened to be there and asked if we were moving back. We responded that we were actually hoping to live up the Blackfoot but couldn't find what we were looking for.

The realtor hosting the open house overheard our conversation and asked what our price range was. After we told him, he said he knew of one that would be available soon that should be about the right price. It was his in-laws' house, and it was in the perfect location, mid-way between the church and Missoula. The owners had asked a reasonable price for the lovely home, but it was $5,000 outside of our comfort zone. We offered what we felt we could afford, knowing fully that the home was worth every dime they were asking for it. They countered our offer with the full price and gave us five days to think about it.

Disappointed, we didn't feel at peace with going any higher, so we began our search once again. I remember praying in the car together that God would lead us to the place He wanted us to live in. We almost settled for another home, but by the time we made up our minds to make an offer on it, they had just signed a buy-sell that very day. We decided we better get back to our realtor one hour before the deadline on the first one and let him know that we couldn't sign the counteroffer for the beautiful home up the Blackfoot. The receptionist had us wait for a moment as the realtor finished up his telephone conversation. When he came out of his office, he told us he had just gotten off the phone with the realtor representing the couple who owned the house we'd fallen in love with. The people had decided to take our original offer, if we were still interested. The price we settled on? One hundred dollars more than what we had sold our current house for! God is always faithful. In the past we sometimes made decisions based on what we wanted rather than waiting for God to open the proper doors. This was a wonderful example of what waiting patiently on the Lord can do.

We made the deal before it ever hit the market and proceeded to move after closing on it in June with the help of all of our church friends.

There were pickups galore and even a very clean, huge, stock trailer. Amazingly, we had all of our belongings moved within a few hours. It's easy to understand why we were so attached to these people.

I applied for a job as a downtown ambassador in August and started in September of 2006. I had actually become re-certified to teach and applied for a few teaching jobs, but nothing came about. I feel very fortunate it turned out the way it did as events unfolded during the coming fall and winter. The stress from being a brand-new teacher in an unfamiliar school and grade level most certainly would have pushed me over the edge.

The job of a downtown ambassador focuses mainly on hospitality, safety, and security. Basically, it is my goal to make downtown a more pleasant place to be. I am also a liason between the police department and business or property owners. Some of my duties include photographing graffiti, dealing with problem behaviors, specifically with panhandlers, working special events from an information cart, and educating folks about city ordinances. It is a very flexible job, and I am treated very well by my employer. At three-quarter time, it is all I would really want at this point.

We planned to attend a Christian concert/motorcycle show in another town with our youth group, so we canvassed our new neighborhood and invited kids to come along. Our next-door neighbors allowed two of their boys to travel with us, and one of them accepted Christ at the concert. I have to admit, I was a bit nervous about what his parents were going to think since we really didn't know them at all or where they stood as far as faith in God. It turned out that, although they were not churchgoers at the time, they were happy about their son's decision and have been coming to our church as a family ever since. Not only that, but they help out in many areas of ministry as well. After thinking God was giving us our new house at a price we could afford in order to bless us, it showed me that He also had a few other things in mind. The neighbors received the blessing of salvation and then passed many blessings on to the church. Then the church passed on blessings to others in the community, and so it continues.

Youth group resumed with regular weekly meetings after the summer break, right about the time I went to work. Since our numbers had grown, we decided to split the youth group into separate junior high and high school nights. It was held in our house, except for special events. I was very excited about the number of kids involved and also how everything seemed to be working out well for us concerning the move and jobs.

I especially felt appreciative of our pastor and his wife for being so welcoming to us during the four years we'd gone to church there. A lot of old wounds had healed. One night I couldn't sleep because the wheels in my head were turning. I finally got up and wrote a poem about our church, specifically about our pastor and his wife. I'm sure I was in a manic state at the time, because it just poured out on the page. I couldn't write fast enough. Then I went to bed.

Welcome and We Love You

Tattered and torn
Weary and worn
Welcome and we love you

Bring all your cares
Worries and fears
Welcome and we love you

Injured and bruised
Damaged and used
Welcome and we love you

We know that the trial
Lasts only a while
Welcome and we love you

Those who need love
There is help from above
Welcome and we love you

God has a reason
For allowing this season
Welcome and we love you

Our Redeemer and friend
Will comfort, guide, and defend
Welcome and we love you

Forgive one another
Let God bind us together
Welcome and we love you

This is a place
Of healing and grace
Welcome and we love you

I had a lot to adjust to after such a quiet life the previous four years. All of a sudden I was working again, and we had taken on more with the youth group than before. Because of Jim's change of position within the police department, he had to miss many of the youth group nights. There always seemed to be a game or some other school event he needed to attend. That meant I was left to plan youth group by myself, for the most part. I was revved up in high gear at the beginning but couldn't sustain it. I started to have what I would call meltdowns approximately once a month. I was rapid-cycling due to increased stress but wasn't aware I had bipolar disorder yet. Thoughts of death invaded my mind on occasion, though I never seriously considered suicide. Out of exhaustion, while driving to work, there were times I would imagine drifting over into the lane of an oncoming semi-truck. Then life, and all its weariness, would finally be over. It was not something I seriously planned to do but was a momentary escape from reality.

In October of that year, a friend of mine told me she had been diagnosed with bipolar disorder. I didn't know what to think about this news. After all, the only time I had ever heard about the illness, the media was reporting about a teacher who had sex with her students or a mom who killed her children. My friend didn't fit either description, so I decided to do some research on my own.

I looked up bipolar disorder online and started to read. As I continued, I felt like I was reading about my own life. There was a test to see if you had any of the characteristics of the illness, so curiosity got the best of me, and I took it. I'm not sure if one would say I passed the test with flying colors or I failed it miserably. What mattered was that it recommended I have an evaluation. This was not at all what I expected when I got on the computer that day. I was nowhere near ready to accept that I might be struggling with a mental illness, but it was something I pondered as I continued to spiral downward.

In October, after only being on the job for a little over a month, I was tempted to quit my new position. I was quite affected by a coworker's negative attitude. Also, a street vendor who was not licensed threw a fit and called my boss because I had spoken with her about the city ordinance that applied to what she was doing. This woman was a bit out of control, though I had only attempted to help her understand what she could do in order to be operating legally. I had quit so many jobs in the past and I did need to have the income, so even though it was an immense struggle, I tried really hard to weather the storm. Eventually both of these situations worked themselves out, and I was glad I stayed. The coworker obtained other employment about a year later, and it felt like a couple hundred pounds of weight dropped off my shoulders. The street vendor drifted out of the picture fairly quickly, and my boss was sympathetic toward me concerning the situation.

At Christmastime, our church has an ornament and cookie exchange and secret pal reveal for the women. I had to work on Saturday that first year back at work, and the pastor's wife, who is a dear friend, called to tell me she didn't think many people were coming to this ladies' event. She was feeling pretty discouraged, and as anyone involved in ministry can attest, sometimes working so hard without much excitement from others can take its toll on a person. She was at that point when I told her I couldn't come because of work either. When she cried, I handled it quite well until the second time we visited about it. Somehow her disappointment that I would not be there hit me pretty hard. It resulted in a serious mental issue for me, as I totally overreacted to how she felt about my absence. I have a hard time letting people I care about down, and I was an absolute mess for a few days. This was really nothing to get so worked up about, but I was in a state of rapid cycling at that point, having major meltdowns close together.

In late January of 2007, Jim and I finally took our honeymoon trip to Maui. Our twenty-fifth wedding anniversary was the previous September, and we had celebrated with a surprise party given by our kids. Throughout our marriage, we had either been too broke or too busy for a honeymoon so we decided it was long overdue. Our vacations throughout the years usually consisted of camping with the boys or finding some other inexpensive destination. I was so excited, I couldn't stand it. We were going to do it up right and spare no expense. It was also the beginning of the season for spotting humpback whales. As a wildlife lover, whether it be on land or in the sea, this was something I was really looking forward to.

Surprise party for our twenty-fifth wedding anniversary,
hosted by our kids, September 2006.

For one reason or another, it seemed every excursion we planned to go on didn't work out. Most of the time we couldn't get out on the water due to extreme wind. With each passing day, I was afraid I wouldn't have the opportunity to get up close and personal with the whales. We resorted to some other outings to try and make the best of things. Jim and I decided to drive up to an inactive volcano when we couldn't go on one of our excursions. It was so windy up there, we could barely push our vehicle doors open to get out of the rental car without having them slam back on our legs. The clouds were resting on top of the opening of the old volcano, so we could not see anything either. We only stayed a few minutes after the long drive up the winding road because standing up was next to impossible as we battled the wind, and it was actually quite cold out. As we drove back down the mountain, re-entering the sunshine, we talked about what we should do with the rest of our day.

Upon returning to our hotel, we decided to go swimming. Our pool was next to the beach, so we had our choice of where we wanted to swim. The people on the beach also had their excursions cancelled, but they didn't leave the area to do anything else. They were so excited because they had seen whales right out in front of our hotel, plus either a seal or sea lion was throwing an eel around in the air, just a matter of fifty yards or so out from where they were sitting. Now the show was over and there were no more animals to be found. I was so disappointed! We had taken that long drive, all for naught, and everyone who stayed to soak in the sunshine had the best time and enjoyed sharing every detail. Maybe that would be the only opportunity to see a whale up close, and I had missed it.

Another day, as a second choice, we ended up taking a bus ride around the island. Our driver had a real chip on his shoulder. It almost seemed as though, as a native Hawaiian, he was angry that all of the vacationers were ruining the island paradise. He said horrible things to some of the passengers and drove like a maniac. He was incredibly rude to a poor woman who was becoming ill from his erratic driving. The driver harshly reprimanded her, lest she actually vomit on his bus, because he was in no mood to clean it up. It was an immensely long twelve hours, but we were trapped. Once on the bus, there was no going back. I was at my breaking point, and it even offended my easygoing husband. Upon our return, I complained to the concierge about the driver but to no avail. We could not be reimbursed for what we had spent on the bus ride, and we certainly could not get those hours back, which was actually the greatest disappointment.

During the rest of our stay, Jim kept telling me to enjoy myself. After all, we weren't at work; we were together in Hawaii where we could relax. I knew I should have had the same attitude, but something inside of me wouldn't allow it. One evening after a very sullen dinner, Jim began to get impatient with me. I was holding my head, trying to will it to behave, saying, "I know I'm being a baby. I'm trying so hard!" I was absolutely pleading with him to give me time and space, but he'd had enough and was quite angry. Out of sheer will and determination, I did improve somewhat, but I wasn't completely myself, so I pretended the best I could.

Believe it or not, the highlight of our trip up to that point was probably when we went to see a magician/comedian, *in Hawaii*. He was the best I've ever seen. We met two other couples on the long bus ride, so we went to this show with them. They were so nice, two pastors and their wives from Idaho, and even seemed to enjoy the trip around the island. I couldn't figure out how they had a good time on that wretched bus. Though I tried not to be, I know I was pretty depressing to hang around during the pre-show dessert. These wonderful people kindly tolerated me as I attempted to fake it. By the time the show was over, though, I was able to shake off my ill-humored mood, since it had temporarily taken my mind off some of the disappointments of the vacation.

We finally were allowed to go out on a boat to see whales the day before we left, and it was amazing! Somehow we ended up in a competition pod, where one female and several male humpback whales were circling our boat at close range. These massive creatures seemed to dwarf our watercraft in an astounding display. The marine biologist explained what was happening and put a microphone in the water so we could listen to their songs. We finally experienced even more than what I initially hoped for, but I went home feeling guilty because I had ruined the long-awaited honeymoon that we had spent so much money on. I understand now that passing through three time zones was at least partially to blame for this episode, but I felt like a rotten person at the time.

Then, to finish off our wonderful vacation, a huge coconut fell from a tree and dented the roof of our rental car prior to returning it and boarding the plane. One last hit, for good measure, but by then at least, I could laugh about it. This kind of put the exclamation point on our entire honeymoon!

CHAPTER 14

THE FAMILY ILLNESS

The Lord is my shepherd, I shall lack nothing. He makes
me lie down in green pastures, he leads me beside quiet
waters, he restores my soul. He guides me in paths of
righteousness for his name's sake. Even though I walk
through the valley of the shadow of death, I will fear
no evil, for you are with me; your rod and your staff,
they comfort me. You prepare a table before me in the
presence of my enemies. You anoint my head with oil;
my cup overflows. Surely goodness and love will follow
me all the days of my life, and I will dwell in the house
of the Lord forever.

—Psalm 23

My mom periodically suggested I take antidepressants since
"depression runs in our family." Obviously, she had observed
signs that something was wrong at various points in my life. I had always
resisted because I felt happiness was a choice. I continually read Bible
verses that spoke of being joyful. Proverbs 17:22 says, "A cheerful heart
is good medicine, but a crushed spirit dries up the bones." If I *chose*
happiness, then I wouldn't need medication. It was as simple as that.
What I failed to realize was that this verse never said medicine was bad;
in fact, it implied it is good! I would never expect a cancer patient or
heart patient to forgo treatment for their medical conditions. Why should
a brain disorder be any different?

I now believe this particular Bible verse has many interpretations.
Stress does cause or exacerbate health conditions, so trying to maintain
a positive attitude is very helpful in life. However, a person with a mental
illness has a huge obstacle in his path, and some sort of treatment may
be necessary to move the boulder out of the way. Life doesn't need to

hurt this much. The important thing to remember is that a pill can't fix everything either, so it is necessary to attend to the spiritual aspects of wellness in addition to the physical ones. One without the other is less effective; I am evidence of that. You may be able to survive while not really living.

The next major meltdown I experienced one month after the trip to Hawaii occurred because of the youth group activity when a girl's comment caused me to desire to cut or burn my flesh. Because of this event, I finally realized I needed help, so Jim and I searched for a professional. At first, I attempted to schedule an appointment with my friend's practitioner, since I'd never been to anyone in the medical field for something like this. It turned out that she was not taking any new patients at that time. Hesitantly, we resorted to looking in the phone book. I knew I needed to find someone who recognized even the most subtle differences between various mental disorders after an experience with my general physician several years earlier. During a routine physical at that time, I told my doctor I had been feeling tired lately. He responded that I should take an antidepressant; after all, what could it hurt? He was extremely insistent. During that period, I was still in a place of believing happiness is always a choice, so I resisted. Now, I am glad I did. He asked no further questions yet wanted to prescribe something to alter my brain chemistry. This is not wise at all because it is of utmost importance to have a proper diagnosis in order to prescribe the most effective treatment.

In a small yellow page ad, I found what I was looking for. A medical professional advertised that she worked with people suffering from things such as obsessive-compulsive disorder, anxiety disorders, depression, and bipolar disorder. My mom repeatedly told me that depression ran in our family, but I had taken the online test that caused me to wonder if I actually suffered from bipolar disorder. I needed to finally know whether I was suffering from one of those two disorders or something else.

After nearly three decades of battling an adversary I didn't know existed, I was about to head in a new direction. My nurse practitioner, Ellen, spent a lengthy amount of time with me. She asked all sorts of questions and listened to my ramblings. After all, where do you begin with a story like mine? At the end of the session, she told me she is very careful about diagnosing bipolar disorder. This is due to the stigma, but she also feels it is over-diagnosed. Ellen would prefer to say someone has bipolar tendencies. In my case, she was certain: I do have manic depressive disorder. The enemy finally had a name, and now we could develop a plan of attack.

My immediate reaction was a mixture of both, "I knew it was this," to "Are you really certain?" There was something about this type of diagnosis that was hard to swallow, even though in my heart I knew it was true.

A lot of different emotions welled up inside of me in the coming days and weeks. I felt a sense of relief, in a way, because now I knew what the opponent was, and there was help. I was so weary and did not have the stamina to keep fighting in the manner I had relied upon for years. I also felt a little bit of shame, unnecessarily, because no one *wants* to have a mental illness. It wasn't something I could be completely open about for a while. I remembered how kids would make jokes on track trips when we passed the state mental hospital in Montana. I didn't want to be one of *those* people.

There was a sadness as I came to grips with the fact that, though there is treatment, it is considered an incurable illness. I would have to live with it the rest of my life. Bipolar disorder robbed me, and my relationships, of such joy throughout adulthood, and I needed to grieve the loss of so many dreams along the way. This was probably the most difficult emotion to deal with. There were so many regrets that it was almost overwhelming. Conversely, I also had a sense of pride since I had been strong enough to endure. It had not defeated me! After all those years of perceived failure, my name truly did fit me: Laurie, crown of victory! Most importantly, I felt gratitude to the Lord, who saved my life and encouraged me through His Word to keep fighting the fight. Without Him, I never could have survived.

The first person I told of my diagnosis was my husband, who was quite skeptical at first. As a police officer, the only people with bipolar disorder he'd dealt with were having extreme episodes. I hadn't stolen a car or run down the street in my underwear, which is what he thought of when referring to bipolar disorder. When he knew he was going on a call that involved someone suffering from this, he would immediately believe he was in for an interesting night, and generally he was right, since the person was in a crisis. I had hidden my worst from him. I informed my biological family next, due to the fact that mental disorders are prevalent within families. It was extremely important for them to receive this knowledge, since we knew of several who had struggled.

When Jim and I told our adult sons, they were wonderfully supportive. I was attempting to explain the disorder to them, so I proceeded to give the most notable example from their childhood when I had thrown their toys away. Garrett, with a grin, said, "You didn't get all of them!" We had a good laugh, realizing our children, though disobedient in this instance, had their own coping mechanisms in place to deal with the occasional craziness. Garrett also told me I had been a good mom. He knew exactly what an insecure mom needed to hear.

It has been a road to recovery ever since the initial diagnosis. A person does not get over years and years of pain overnight. The following November, I made another appointment with a plastic surgeon to discuss having a breast augmentation. I chose a different physician from the first time, and I was pleased that his philosophy was to keep me looking as natural as possible by not going with too large of implants. I was so comfortable with this doctor that I scheduled the surgery for January. From the November examination forward, I wrestled over the path I was choosing. One day I would feel one way, and the next day I would feel the opposite. I wanted to finally be able to shop for clothes and feel like I looked attractive in them, yet I had some nagging doubts.

As a youth group leader, what message would I be sending to impressionable teenage girls about how they felt about their own bodies? What would God feel about this decision I was making? After all, I would basically be saying I wasn't satisfied with how He created me. Would it be a sin to follow through, or would it be no big deal? Since I was still contending with these mixed feelings in January, I canceled the procedure. There have been periods when I've reconsidered my choice in the months and years following, but at this time, I am still not at peace with going ahead. My husband has encouraged me that he is completely satisfied with me just exactly the way I am, and I have come a long way in self-acceptance.

With the passing of time, I have become more and more candid about my diagnosis. I told trusted friends and continued from there as I found that people, though quite surprised to find out I suffered from bipolar disorder, were always very supportive. Now I speak to groups and openly share about my experiences. Each time I choose to tell my secret, I gain confidence and strength. I've also found there are far more people with brain disorders than I ever realized. Often people do not speak about a mental disorder until they feel safe. It is the secret no one wants to share but at the same time, may desperately need to share. It is a lonely enough life for the afflicted that further isolation because of the diagnosis could be detrimental. At least for me it would be. One must be sufficiently far along in the acceptance and healing process, however, to divulge such a secret. It is a gradual happening that should be dictated by the person who is dealing with his own diagnosis.

Understanding that Jim needed freedom to share with trusted friends as he was adjusting to the news of this disorder, I only requested that he check with me before he told others. He did choose to reveal it to a few people without my knowledge. I wasn't comfortable with some of them having that information about me and felt a bit betrayed at first. I know Jim meant no harm, and he felt at ease with the ones he spoke with. It would have been nice to have been consulted beforehand, but at this point in time, I experience such freedom from being open that I don't care who knows about it.

My grandmother had what was referred to as a "chemical imbalance" in her brain. She was a wonderful, caring person, and I loved to visit her as a child. I knew she struggled with depression, however, from things I heard family members say. Unfortunately for her, treatment options were not as sophisticated as they are now. She endured shock treatments and they experimented with many different medications, but she never enjoyed the success I have with my treatment plan. Several other relatives have been on antidepressants. There has been substance abuse in my extended family as well, which can be a sign of self-medication. Since my diagnosis, it has been concluded that two other family members have bipolar disorder. Then there was my sweet nephew, Jeremy.

Grandma Rush

Jeremy was never diagnosed with bipolar disorder, but I always felt we had some very similar traits. He loved animals and children, was a distance runner who broke four minutes in the mile, and was also a very good student. Though a bit impulsive at times, he had a personality everyone was drawn to, always putting others first. How could a person not love someone like Jeremy? He tended to give all of himself in relationships but would easily be heartbroken. That's actually one of the factors that led to his untimely death and nearly led to mine so many years ago. If only he'd known what value he had to so many people and what a bright future could have been his. Unfortunately, he was incapable of seeing beyond his pain.

After Jeremy took his life in 2003, my sister let me read his journal. I completely understood him and am convinced this precious life was taken by manic depressive disorder. We will never know for sure, but it seems quite likely. Because of losing Jeremy and experiencing all I have in life, it is now my goal to help others who may be afflicted or are living with someone who is afflicted with a mental illness. It is no longer something that needs to be hidden. It is not shameful. The only thing that is a shame is the fact that people are suffering needlessly when help is available.

Of concern to me in the future, of course, is the well-being of my sons and their children. As long as our communication is open and we maintain a high level of awareness, I believe we can alleviate a lot of suffering in those family members who may develop signs of this illness in years to come. It is common for it to show itself in a person's late teens to early twenties, though it is certainly not restricted to that time-frame. Understanding the potential triggers is vitally important in determining how to manage this illness.

Being aware of what the symptoms are for bipolar disorder is so critical, especially if it has already shown up in a family member. There tends to be a genetic link, as we have certainly found in my family. Bipolar disorder is marked by dramatic and unpredictable mood swings. I was diagnosed with bipolar I, which means I have had at least one manic episode where my abnormally elevated mood caused a behavior that disrupted my life. Unfortunately, there have been several occurrences of this in my lifetime. Bipolar II is a bit more subdued in that a full-blown mania is not ever reached. Ten to 20 percent of those suffering from bipolar disorder also experience something called rapid cycling. This is when there are four or more episodes of mania or depression within one year. I am one of the unlucky ones to also fit in this category. A mixed episode is when both mania and depression present simultaneously or in rapid succession. This too is something I have suffered from and is when a person is most at risk of suicide. When someone is truly depressed, often he or she does not have the energy to follow through by taking his or her own life. Depression coupled with the high anxiety of a manic episode can create a deadly situation.

Some complications of bipolar disorder involve self-injury. Included are things like cutting, self-mutilation, and other forms of self-harm. Self-injury can be used as a ritual or as an immediate release in a time of stress. Some types of this include picking at skin, head banging, burning, scratching, pulling hair out, hitting, or biting. As I've shared throughout my story, I experienced some of these to varying degrees as far back as the primary grades and of course struggled with the ultimate self-injury of suicide. It is estimated that between 25 and 50 percent of people with bipolar disorder attempt suicide, while as many as 20 percent of sufferers complete the act.

Along with the professional help of medication, my mood is greatly impacted by food choices, sleep patterns, and exercise. There is a commonly held belief that consuming fish regularly or taking daily fish oil supplements helps with brain function. Eating a variety of nuts may also be beneficial for the same reason. Consuming a diet low in fat and sodium but high in lean meats, fruits, and vegetables seems to be helpful for me in maintaining a balanced mood. I also tend to drink a lot of water and eat regular meals, including breakfast, so I maintain energy throughout the day. People often know a period of mania is on its way due to the inability to sleep at night. A couple of things I've found helpful are to exercise regularly but not too near bedtime and to take melatonin, a natural sleep aid, when I know I really need to have a restful night. Regular sleep patterns are critical for someone like me.

Coming to terms with my limitations has been no easy task. I've found it wisest to learn to live within them, however, since the benefits are significant. It has been especially difficult to be limited in how much I can accomplish each day. For someone who used to feel like I could conquer the world without being held back, I have learned to take time to rest when I sense I am nearing the edge. Knowledge is power, and it is my desire to live an empowered life.

Jim's family had another reunion about two years after I found out I had a mental illness. This time, it was wonderful, and I had so much fun with all of his sisters. The amazing thing was, they did not yet know I had suffered from bipolar disorder for my entire adult life. What this reunion revealed to me is that my level of wellness dictated to a great extent how well I related to others. They hadn't changed, but I had. I am so pleased with this result and feel like it helped with the healing process from past wounds. Quite possibly I was more to blame for the dysfunction from my past than anyone else. For someone who always wanted to place blame on others when my mind was ill, this was a huge revelation. I am happy with how improved all of my relationships have become, and I expect a very bright future. Realizing

I am only responsible for my own decisions also causes me to feel very empowered.

The recent passing of another anniversary date since my diagnosis with bipolar disorder caused me to reflect on God's goodness and faithfulness. He made a promise to me twenty-six years prior to my diagnosis that I would be happy again. Even though the news that I suffered with bipolar disorder was not entirely welcome at the moment and I still had a long way to go in the healing process, it was the beginning of the fulfillment of God's promise to me. Isn't it amazing how God works? Probably no one could have predicted that finding out I had bipolar disorder would be the way God would finally answer my agonizing prayer of two simple words so many years ago: "Help me!" Oh, how He did help me, sustain me, love me, and heal my broken heart. His love truly has followed me all the days of my life, even when I couldn't always see it.

CHAPTER 15

NEW HOPE

"For I know the plans I have for you," declares the Lord, "plans to prosper you and not to harm you, plans to give you hope and a future. Then you will call upon me and come and pray to me, and I will listen to you. You will seek me and find me when you seek me with all your heart. I will be found by you," declares the Lord, "and will bring you back from captivity"
—Jeremiah 29:11–14a

Rediscovering myself has been an exciting time. Writing this book was an integral part of the process, involving a gradual healing from the point of diagnosis to now. I needed to re-evaluate each of the situations that caused me great pain and see them with new eyes and a healthy mind. While this exercise can be terribly uncomfortable, I've found it necessary in order to move forward. The purpose of writing is for healing, understanding, forgiveness, and hope, not ruining relationships. It is my true desire that I have been successful.

I am exceedingly thankful for my husband and have realized how incredibly blessed I am. He has been so understanding and compassionate since we found out about this illness and has done his best to learn what he can do to help me. Jim attended the NAMI (National Alliance for the Mentally Ill) twelve-week Family-to-Family program and benefited so much that he became trained as a leader. He recently assisted his second group as they walked through the same learning process that helped us so much. Jim's laid-back nature I fell in love with from the beginning has been extremely beneficial for me as I have come to grips with the role this disorder has played in my life. I have learned not to expect so much of myself, and he has picked up the slack. When I need a day to relax, he'll take over. I should have acquired this knowledge years ago! I've never felt more loved and accepted than I do right now.

Jim had heart surgery in December of 2010. It was the second procedure he's had done to attempt to fix his atrial fibrillation. The first time, we traveled to Los Angeles for ten days because a particular surgeon was highly recommended to us. Out of the approximately 250 procedures this doctor performs each year, he only has one or two complications, on average. We never dreamed anything could go wrong, but Jim was the one patient who suffered from a complication that year. After only 10 percent of the surgery was completed, the wall of his heart was perforated. The doctor had to stop what he was doing to drain the blood from between that and the pericardium, which is the casing around the heart. This is an extremely serious complication that could have ended with a very negative result, had it been a less skilled physician.

Alone in the waiting room for hours with no update, I started to become concerned. Far too much time had passed, and there was still no word. Finally the doctor came in and said, "Why don't we sit down?" My first thought was, *What did you do to him, kill him?* Instead of leaving the hospital the next day, Jim was in intensive care, feeling the worst he has ever felt in his entire life. He had to lay uncomfortably flat on his back. Otherwise the bleeding could worsen. Unfortunately, after much pain and thousands of dollars later, he still had the same problem with his heart.

A couple of years went by, and Jim decided he was ready to look into a new procedure to address the heart condition he inherited from both of his parents. This time he went to a wonderful doctor at our very own heart institute in Missoula. I was supported by family and friends who sat with me during the entire procedure, and the nursing staff continually gave me updates on how it was progressing. The communication here at home was incredible and showed me how much it was lacking in Los Angeles. We did not feel like a number here. Once the procedure was completed and the surgeon came to the waiting room to talk to me, he was so thorough and kind while explaining everything. After he was done speaking, I thanked him and began to cry. After our experience in LA, it was an enormous relief. I hadn't realized quite how nervous I was about losing Jim on the operating table until that very moment. As I look back at our life together as husband and wife, everything has remarkably changed. I have gone from feeling trapped and lonely to not knowing how I would ever manage without my life partner. He is most certainly God's gift to me.

After a history of difficulty traveling through time zones, I was afraid I would never have the courage to travel to New Zealand and Australia. Experiencing the varied flora and fauna is appealing to me and has been a lifelong dream, one I hope to fulfill in the future. An extreme situation prompted me to cross numerous time zones in April of 2010. My niece in Finland had given birth to twin micro-preemies, and at only twenty-four weeks, five days gestation, they weighed less than two pounds each. My sister wanted to support her in person, so I volunteered to make the trip with her. Finland is nine time zones from Montana, and I handled the extremely stressful situation better than I ever could have imagined. I consulted my nurse practitioner before leaving so I could appropriately modify my medication plan to suit the time change. She had total confidence that I would have a successful trip. I exercised daily while there because I dared not become a liability in this situation. It was a huge triumph for me, and I was excited to learn it is no longer necessary to be fearful of realizing my dream of seeing kangaroos and koala if the opportunity arises. Not all of my childhood aspirations need to die because of this disorder!

My niece and her beautiful family in Finland, 2010.

Some people struggle with staying on their medications for a variety of reasons, but I am very committed to following orders. After spending decades utilizing every possible coping mechanism, though helpful, I was still not completely well. Since receiving a diagnosis, I have not failed to take the medications prescribed to me. Initially, I was given a mood stabilizer, which by itself made me feel lethargic. All I wanted to do that first summer was to come home from work, go down in the cool, dark basement, and watch TV. It was extremely out of character for me, and I contacted Ellen after I had given it a fair chance to see the effects.

I am very proactive in my treatment plan because I want to be well. After all, I didn't struggle so hard all those years to give up now. When suffering from a mental disorder, it takes great motivation to obtain the most life has to offer. This is not always easy, but is essential for optimal health. I did some research and wondered if adding an antidepressant might help me feel better. Ellen agreed and prescribed a low-dose medication, which has worked wonders. Again, there was an adjustment period, but I feel much better than I did. I doubt I will ever have the energy I once had, partly due to aging and partly due to having my mania under control, but it is better than the alternative.

A slight amount of weight gain is evident, due to the medications, but it is something I have chosen to accept. Another somewhat noticeable side effect is hair loss. I began finding a lot of hair in my brush and on the bathroom floor, but a nurse friend told me to take vitamin B12. I'm not bald yet, so it must be working! Due to taking a mood stabilizer, I have slight tremors in my hands, but it has not posed a problem. These minor inconveniences pale in comparison to the previous unrest I routinely experienced.

Besides professional help and loving support from my family, there are many things to which I attribute my overall wellness. It is necessary to take care of oneself physically. Eating right, getting enough sleep, and exercising on a routine basis are essential. Staying away from alcohol or drugs is helpful. I've come to realize I don't have to be perfect in appearance, intelligence, or talent, but loving God and loving people are enough. Not expecting others to be perfect is also valuable when there is a need to forgive. Praying, reading God's Word, attending a fellowship of believers, and listening to uplifting, meaningful Christian music have literally been life-saving for me.

In my position as a downtown ambassador, I am required to address certain problem behaviors I come across. Often these situations involve homeless people with drug or alcohol addiction problems and sometimes mental health issues. Though some of the behaviors cannot be tolerated, the people can be. Due to my personal awareness of what it feels like to struggle from a mental illness, I believe it causes me to be much more effective in my current position. If I hadn't had a stable family to grow up in or if certain situations had been different along the way, I could have ended up without a job or support system. Maybe I would have also chosen alcohol to help me get through the day and numb the pain. I am constantly reminded that by the grace of God, I have what I have and can enjoy a happy, fulfilled, successful life. A few different circumstances and I could have ended up homeless and hopeless.

I treat people on the street as I would want to be treated—with dignity and respect. In return, they generally treat me the same way. However, this can be a very dangerous job since one never knows where people are from or what they have done in their lives, and I only carry pepper spray. I know many homeless folks carry knives and other weapons, and I can't blame them. It is unsafe living out there, especially at night. I simply put my faith in the Lord's protection, treat people with respect and compassion, watch my back, and wear my running shoes!

As I look back at all that Jim and I have been through in our years together, there is one recurring theme. There is always hope for reconciliation and forgiveness if your heart is open to it. I am so fortunate to have a loving husband who did not give up on me. He definitely made a few mistakes as a young man that truly hurt me, but it is important to be aware that a person with bipolar disorder feels things much more vividly than others. Things that are positive become even better and more exciting, but things that hurt become devastating. My responses were affected due to this fact. I changed into the needy girl in our dating and early married years—the girl I didn't like. I was desperate and moody, sacrificing everything while becoming bitter about the result. Just the other day, Jim said, "I made a lot of mistakes in the past, but I never cheated on you." And I can finally say that I believe him. All those years of suspicion and doubt were so damaging to each of us, but it makes the present that much sweeter. It is wonderful to be in a loving and trusting relationship, and is something I do not take for granted.

Being well after such a long time is nothing short of miraculous. Many people lose everything, including their families, health, finances, and even their lives to this disorder. God has blessed me in that I somehow kept these things intact, but I didn't do it alone.

Jim and I are having the most fun at this stage of our lives. We have matured and grown together, rather than apart, through all of the difficulties. I enjoy his company and think he is the kindest, funniest person I've ever known. This is a relationship that is ever-changing, and I am never bored. We are very close to our sons and their families and spend more time socially with them than anyone else. This is due in large part to what an entertaining and loving person Jim is. We now have a daughter-in-law, Leah, and our other son is engaged to Fawn. I love these girls like they are my own, and we can talk about anything. Now we have a new little grandson, Brent Andrew James Johnson, born on September 30, 2011. Being able to share my life with Jim couldn't be better, and I can see how God has sustained us through everything to get to this place in life. It is interesting to look back at our journey and see how God had His hand on us every step of the way. He even had a plan way back when our parents each brought their families to a little town in Montana.

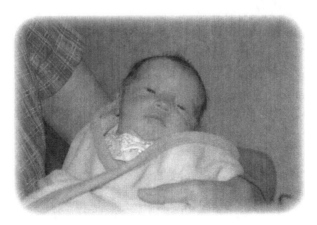

Our grandson, Brent Andrew James Johnson.

Garrett and Leah at their wedding, December 2007.

Chad and his fiancée, Fawn.

Our family photo, December 2010.

Years ago my dreams centered around what I could accomplish in track and my career. I now realize there are many things that are more important than fame and fortune. My desire is to openly share my experiences and how God met me at each turn in order to encourage others. After several speaking engagements, I am finding that my desire to give others hope has grown stronger and stronger. Recently, while speaking to a group of high school students, I was asked, "Do you feel you have been dealt a lame hand by God?" I told them I would be lying if the thought had never crossed my mind, but the answer is no. I believe God allows trials in our lives to help us learn to trust Him, to mature and develop character, and to help and encourage others who are struggling. I felt that way about my son dying, and I feel the same about bipolar disorder.

Each difficult circumstance I've endured has been beneficial in some way. I am to use whatever God has allowed in my life to bring glory and honor to Him. There will be opportunities for growth during the rest of my days, because God is never done teaching us. The nicest part for me is that life doesn't feel impossible anymore. Oh, and just as God promised so many years ago, I *am* happy again! I believe that is what He desires for every person He has created.

> But let all who take refuge in you be glad; let them ever sing for joy. Spread your protection over them, that those who love your name may rejoice in you. For surely, O Lord, you bless the righteous; you surround them with your favor as with a shield.
>
> —Psalm 5:11–12

SOME CLOSING THOUGHTS FROM JIM

It is amazing to me how Laurie somehow made it through life while suffering from bipolar I without knowing that she had this mental illness. I have learned so much about this disorder since Laurie made a self-diagnosis over four years ago. I have discovered that mental illness is actually a physical disease and affects millions of Americans. My wish is that through this book, others who are suffering from a mental illness will see there is hope and that they can be helped with medication and counseling. I strongly urge anyone who has a family member with a mental illness to research and obtain as much information as possible. The National Alliance for the Mentally Ill (NAMI) is a great place to start. They offer a Family-to-Family class that is twelve weeks long and really helps people to better understand their family member's illness. I have taken the class myself, and after attending training, I now teach it to others.

After Laurie was officially diagnosed, our life together has steadily improved as we have seen her make huge strides on her road to recovery. She is at a place in her life where she can trust me and other people again and is not totally devastated by a rude comment or action. It is really great that I can tell her anything without fear of her taking it wrong and becoming suspicious. I was especially impressed when she was verbally attacked by someone while on a trip. She stayed calm, and it did not push her into a manic episode. Before her diagnosis and medication, this could have easily turned into a very stressful incident.

I have read that people with bipolar disorder are usually very intelligent, driven, and capable of amazing things. In our relationship, Laurie is the brains of the outfit, and she can do anything she sets her mind to. In her current position with the business improvement district, she has been selected as the Downtown Employee of the Year.

This is due to an incredible work ethic and her ability to effectively communicate with business owners and members of the public. Laurie is well-respected by everyone she works with, including the transient population with whom she deals every day. They all know her by her first name, and I am confident if she were being attacked, the street people would come to her aid.

Laurie has been an incredible mother to our two sons and also to our son Brent, who died at the age of eight and a half months. She was always there for our boys and made sure that they were well-fed and neatly dressed. Garrett and Chad have a deep love for their mother and are very devoted to her. Laurie and I are now enjoying our first grandson and are excited to have a little one in the house for Christmas this year.

As I said earlier, our life as a married couple just gets better every day, and we are fully enjoying each other for the first time in our marriage. It is so good to know Laurie is getting good sleep, not lying awake at night with her mind racing. I am so proud of my beautiful and talented wife and consider myself to be a very lucky man to have her as my life partner. God is so good. Even though we went through some hard times in the early years, I know that the Lord put us together, and His will has been done. We are a living testament that you can go through very rough times and still make it. We are a team now, and I believe we can handle anything the world throws at us.

My hope is that after reading this book, you will see that there is help out there if you are suffering from a mental illness. With treatment, you can have a happy life. If you are experiencing suicidal thoughts or are depressed, please go to a counselor or hospital and ask for help. There are a lot of people out there who care, and you can be well again. If you have a family member who is at risk, please get him or her the assistance he or she needs. Don't give up until you are sure your loved one is being helped and is safe. If your family member will not agree to see a professional, and you feel he or she is a danger to him or herself or others, contact your county attorney and ask for an involuntary commitment. This will get your loved one into a facility for an emergency evaluation.

I want to thank you for reading Laurie's book. I know she wrote it with love and devotion for others who are battling to beat this disease, just trying to live another day. I would also like to thank Laurie for sharing her heart and her life with you. This was a tremendous undertaking for her that took a great deal of time and energy to complete. It has also helped her heal from old wounds she lived with for many years.

ABOUT THE AUTHOR

Laurie Johnson was born in Sioux Falls, South Dakota, the youngest of six children. At an early age, she moved with her family to Missoula, Montana, where she currently resides with her husband of thirty years. They have two grown sons, a daughter-in-law, a future daughter-in-law, and a grandson.

Laurie attended Montana State University, where she competed in track and cross country, until marrying and returning to Missoula. She finished her undergraduate work at the University of Montana and received her BA in elementary education in 1991.

Currently, Laurie is a downtown ambassador for the business improvement district of Missoula. Her ultimate goal is to minister to people with brain disorders and offer a message of hope through her writing and speaking engagements. She would also like to help end the stigma associated with mental illness by sharing her story with the general public on this very important topic.

Laurie is available to speak at schools, churches, mental health organizations, clubs, and conferences. For information on having her for your group contact her via email at iamlauriebook@gmail.com or view her website at www.iamlauriebook.com

ACKNOWLEDGMENTS

A Special Thanks To:

My dear friend Susie, for encouraging me to write my book when I didn't know if it was worthwhile.

My sister-in-law Penna, who read many versions of the manuscript and believed in the message strongly enough to urge me to finish what I started.

My family and friends who gave feedback on how I could improve it. Thank you Mom, Dad, Garrett, Leah, Chad, Fawn, Vicky, Alyssa, Judy, Deaette, Beth, Sarah, Kelli, Shannon, Chris, Brenda, Patty, and Doris for your reassurance and advice.

My children, Garrett and Chad, for growing up to be fine young men in spite of their mother's mistakes, and also for believing I've been a good mom.

My husband, Jim, who has walked this journey with me. Thanks for not giving up on me. I love you with all of my heart.

NOTES

Chapter 5

1. *Jesus Loves Me*, a poem written by Anna Bartlett Warner included in an 1860 book by Susan Warner titled *Say and Seal*, was set to music by William Batchelder Bradbury in 1862. Bradbury also added the chorus, "Yes, Jesus loves me."

Chapter 12

1. *Old Yeller* (1957) is a Walt Disney Productions film about a boy and a stray dog in post-Civil War Texas. The story is based upon the 1956 book *Old Yeller* by Fred Gipson, which won the Newbery Award. Gipson and William Tunberg co-wrote the screenplay.

2. *The Sound of Music* (1959) is a musical based on the memoir of Maria von Trapp, *The Story of the Trapp Family Singers*. Music is by Richard Rodgers, lyrics by Oscar Hammerstein II, and a book is by Howard Lindsay and Russel Crouse.

RESOURCES

American Psychiatric Association (APA)
1000 Wilson Blvd.
Suite 1825
Arlington, VA 22209
703-907-7300
www.healthyminds.org

Depression and Bipolar Support Alliance (DBSA)
730 N. Franklin Street
Suite 501
Chicago, IL 60610-7224
800-826-3632
www.dbsalliance.org

National Alliance for the Mentally Ill (NAMI)
Colonial Place Three
2107 Wilson Blvd., Suite 300
Arlington, VA 22201-3042
703-524-7600
Information Helpline:
800-950-NAMI (6264)
www.nami.org

National Mental Health Association (NMHA)
2001 N. Beauregard Street
12th Floor
Alexandria, VA 22311
800-969-NMHA (6642)
www.nmha.org

National Institute of Mental Health: www.nimh.nih.gov

Center for Disease Control and Prevention: www.cdc.gov/scientific.htm

American Foundation for Suicide Prevention (AFSP): www.afsp.org

National Suicide Prevention Lifeline
1-800-273-TALK

CPSIA information can be obtained at www.ICGtesting.com
Printed in the USA
LVOW08s2158251214

420365LV00015B/132/P